AMERICAN
BAKING
HERITAGE

AMERICAN BAKING HERITAGE

Patricia Lousada

SMITHMARK

This edition published in 1996
by Smithmark Publishers,
a division of U.S. Media Holdings, Inc.,
16 East 32nd Street
New York
NY 10016

SMITHMARK books are available for bulk purchase for sales promotion
and premium use. For details write or call the manager of special sales,
SMITHMARK Publishers
16 East 32nd Street
New York
NY 10016
(212) 532-6600

ISBN 0-8317-5784-1

Publisher: Joanna Lorenz
Senior Cookery Editor: Linda Fraser
Junior Editor: Emma Brown
Designer: Sheila Volpe
Jacket Designer: Adrian Morris
Special Jacket Photography: Patrick McLeavey
Photography and Styling: Amanda Heywood
Food Styling: Elizabeth Wolf-Cohen and Carla Capalbo

Printed in Singapore by Star Standard Industries Pte. Ltd.

10 9 8 7 6 5 4 3 2 1

CONTENTS

~

INTRODUCTION

~

Nothing equals the satisfaction of home baking. No commercial cake mix or store-bought cookie can match one that is made from the best fresh ingredients with all the added enjoyment that baking at home provides – the enticing aromas that fill the house and stimulate appetites, the delicious straight-from-the-oven flavor, as well as the pride of having created such wonderful goodies yourself. *American Baking Heritage* brings the rich history of American baking together in one comprehensive, inspiring collection of baked goods. German, Austrian, French and Italian influences, among others, can be traced in the wide variety of colorful and delicious cookies, muffins, breads, pies, tarts and cakes within these pages.

As you explore the recipes you will come across dishes that bring back the happiest memories – of warm cookies after school, triple layer extravaganza birthday cakes, Sunday treat coffee cakes and much more.

Each dish is clearly explained with step-by-step photographs to help you recreate it successfully. In addition, the following simple guidelines will greatly reduce the possibility of error, no matter how new you are to baking; it is an exact science and needs to be approached in an ordered way. First read through the recipe from beginning to end. Set out all the required ingredients before you begin. Large eggs are assumed unless specified otherwise, and they should be at room temperature for best results. Sift the flour from a fair height – it will have more chance to aerate and lighten.

When a recipe calls for folding one ingredient into another, it should be done in a way that incorporates as much air as possible into the mixture. Use either a large metal spoon or a long rubber or plastic scraper. Gently plunge the spoon or scraper deep into the center of the mixture and, scooping up a large amount of the mixture, fold it over. Turn the bowl slightly so each scoop folds over another part of the mixture.

No two ovens are alike. Buy a reliable oven thermometer and test the temperature of your oven. When possible, bake in the center of the oven where the heat is more likely to be constant. If using a convection oven, follow manufacturer's instructions for baking. Good quality baking pans can improve your results, as they conduct heat more efficiently.

Practice, patience, and enthusiasm are the keys to confident and successful baking. *American Baking Heritage* will inspire you to start sifting flour, breaking eggs and stirring up all sorts of delectable homemade treats – all guaranteed to bring satisfaction to both the baker and those lucky enough to enjoy the results.

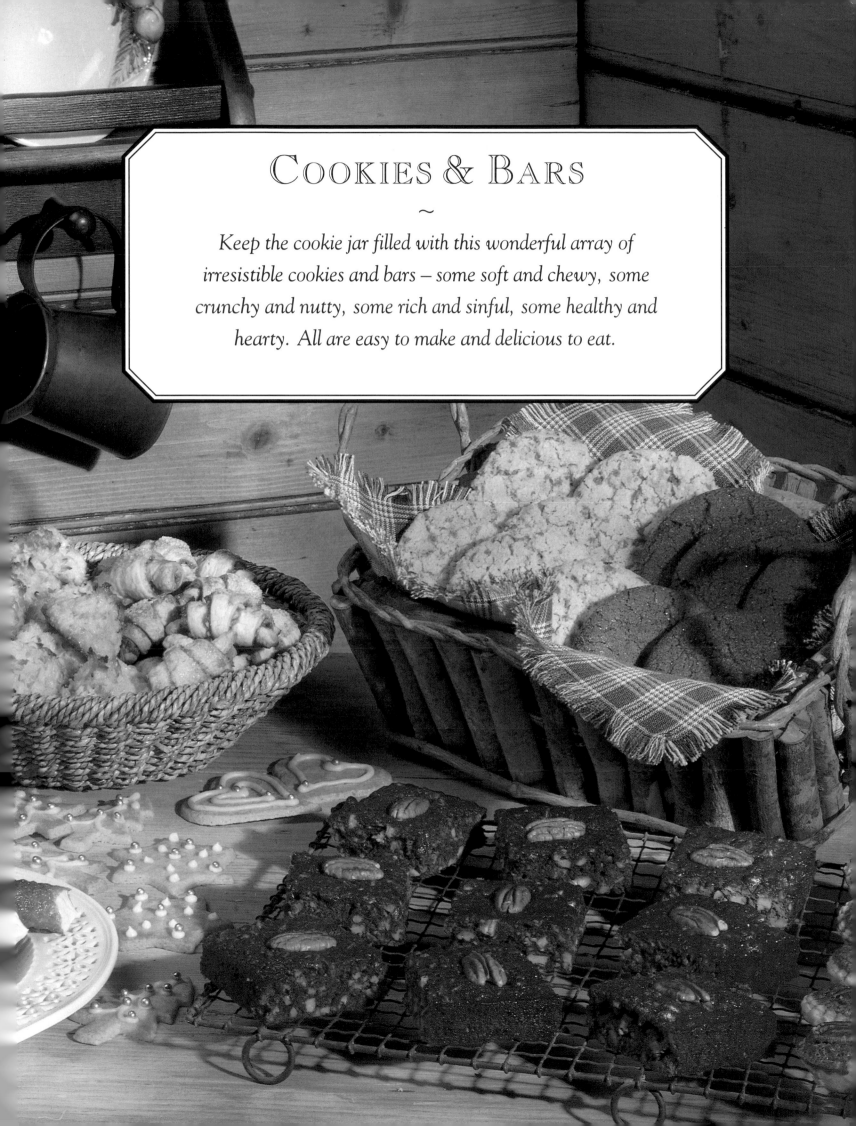

COOKIES & BARS

~

Keep the cookie jar filled with this wonderful array of irresistible cookies and bars – some soft and chewy, some crunchy and nutty, some rich and sinful, some healthy and hearty. All are easy to make and delicious to eat.

Granola Cookies

MAKES 18

½ cup (1 stick) butter or margarine, at room temperature

½ cup light brown sugar, firmly packed

⅓ cup crunchy peanut butter

1 egg

½ cup flour

½ teaspoon baking powder

½ teaspoon cinnamon

⅛ teaspoon salt

2 cups granola cereal

⅓ cup raisins

½ cup walnuts, chopped

1 Preheat oven to 350°F. Grease a cookie sheet.

2 With an electric mixer, cream the butter or margarine and sugar until light and fluffy. Beat in the peanut butter. Beat in the egg.

3 ▲ Sift the flour, baking powder, cinnamon, and salt over the peanut butter mixture and stir to blend. Stir in the granola, raisins, and walnuts. Taste the mixture to see if it needs more sugar, as granolas vary.

4 ▲ Drop rounded tablespoonfuls of the batter onto the prepared cookie sheet about 1 inch apart. Press gently with the back of a spoon to spread each mound into a circle.

5 Bake until lightly colored, about 15 minutes. With a metal spatula, transfer to a rack to cool. Store in an airtight container.

Oatmeal and Cereal Cookies

MAKES 14

¾ cup (1½ sticks) butter or margarine, at room temperature

¾ cup sugar

1 egg yolk

1½ cups flour

1 teaspoon baking soda

½ teaspoon salt

½ cup rolled oats

½ cup small crunchy nugget cereal

~ **VARIATION** ~

For Nutty Oatmeal Cookies, substitute an equal quantity of chopped walnuts or pecans for the cereal, and prepare as described.

1 ▲ With an electric mixer, cream the butter or margarine and sugar together until light and fluffy. Mix in the egg yolk.

2 Sift over the flour, baking soda, and salt, then stir into the butter mixture. Add the oats and cereal and stir to blend. Refrigerate for at least 20 minutes.

3 Preheat the oven to 375°F. Grease a cookie sheet.

4 ▲ Roll the dough into balls. Place them on the cookie sheet and flatten with the bottom of a floured glass.

5 Bake until golden, 10–12 minutes. With a metal spatula, transfer to a rack to cool completely. Store in an airtight container.

Granola Cookies (top), Oatmeal and Cereal Cookies

Ginger Cookies

MAKES 36

1 cup granulated sugar

½ cup light brown sugar, firmly packed

½ cup (1 stick) butter, at room temperature

½ cup (1 stick) margarine, at room temperature

1 egg

⅓ cup molassses

2¼ cups flour

2 teaspoons ground ginger

½ teaspoon grated nutmeg

1 teaspoon ground cinnamon

2 teaspoons baking soda

½ teaspoon salt

1 Preheat the oven to 325°F. Line 2–3 cookie sheets with wax paper and grease lightly.

2 ▲ With an electric mixer, cream ½ cup of the granulated sugar, the brown sugar, butter, and margarine until light and fluffy. Add the egg and continue beating to blend well. Add the molasses.

3 ▲ Sift the dry ingredients 3 times, then stir into the butter mixture. Refrigerate for 30 minutes.

4 ▲ Place the remaining sugar in a shallow dish. Roll tablespoonfuls of the dough into balls, then roll the balls in the sugar to coat.

5 Place the balls 2 inches apart on the prepared sheets and flatten slightly. Bake until golden around the edges but soft in the middle, 12–15 minutes. Let stand for 5 minutes before transferring to a rack to cool.

~ VARIATION ~

To make Gingerbread Men, increase the amount of flour by ¼ cup. Roll out the dough and cut out shapes with a special cutter. Decorate with icing, if wished.

Christmas Cookies

MAKES 30

¾ cup (1½ sticks) unsalted butter, at room temperature

1¼ cups sugar

1 egg

1 egg yolk

1 teaspoon vanilla extract

grated rind of 1 lemon

¼ teaspoon salt

2½ cups flour

FOR DECORATING (OPTIONAL)

colored icing and small candies such as silver balls, red hots, colored sugar sprinkles, etc.

1 ▲ With an electric mixer, cream the butter until soft. Add the sugar gradually and continue beating until light and fluffy.

2 ▲ Using a wooden spoon, slowly mix in the whole egg and the egg yolk. Add the vanilla, lemon rind and salt. Stir to mix well.

3 Add the flour and stir to blend. Gather the dough into a ball, wrap, and refrigerate for 30 minutes.

4 ▼ Preheat the oven to 375°F. On a floured surface, roll out the dough about ⅛ inch thick.

5 ▲ Stamp out shapes or rounds with cookie cutters.

6 Bake until lightly colored, about 8 minutes. Transfer to a rack and let cool completely before decorating, if wished, with icing and candies.

Chocolate Pretzels

MAKES 28

1 cup flour

⅛ teaspoon salt

3 tablespoons unsweetened cocoa powder

½ cup (1 stick) butter, at room temperature

⅔ cup sugar

1 egg

1 egg white, lightly beaten, for glazing

sugar crystals, for sprinkling

1 Sift together the flour, salt and cocoa powder. Set aside. Grease 2 cookie sheets.

2 ▲ With an electric mixer, cream the butter until light. Add the sugar and continue beating until light and fluffy. Beat in the egg. Add the dry ingredients and stir to blend. Gather the dough into a ball, wrap in wax paper, and refrigerate for 1 hour or freeze for 30 minutes.

3 ▲ Roll the dough into 28 small balls. If the dough is sticky, flour your hands. Refrigerate the balls until needed. Preheat the oven to 375°F.

4 ▲ Roll each ball into a rope about 10 inches long. With each rope, form a loop with the two ends facing you. Twist the ends and fold back on to the circle, pressing in to make a pretzel shape. Place on the prepared sheets.

5 ▲ Brush the pretzels with the egg white. Sprinkle sugar crystals over the tops and bake until firm, 10–12 minutes. Transfer to a rack to cool.

Cream Cheese Spirals

MAKES 32

1 cup (2 sticks) butter, at room
   temperature

8 ounces cream cheese

2 teaspoons granulated sugar

2 cups flour

1 egg white beaten with 1 tablespoon
   water, for glazing

granulated sugar, for sprinkling

FOR THE FILLING

1 cup walnuts or pecans, finely chopped

½ cup light brown sugar, firmly packed

1 teaspoon ground cinnamon

1 With an electric mixer, cream the
butter, cream cheese, and sugar until
soft. Sift over the flour and mix to
form a dough. Gather into a ball and
divide in half. Flatten each half, wrap
in wax paper and refrigerate for at
least 30 minutes.

2 Meanwhile, make the filling. Mix
together the chopped walnuts or
pecans, the brown sugar, and the
cinnamon. Set aside.

3 Preheat the oven to 375°F. Grease
2 cookie sheets.

4 ▲ Working with one half of the
dough at a time, roll out thinly into a
circle about 11 inches in diameter.
Trim the edges with a knife, using a
dinner plate as a guide.

5 ▼ Brush the surface with the egg
white glaze and sprinkle the dough
evenly with half the filling.

6 Cut the dough into quarters, and
each quarter into 4 sections, to form
16 triangles.

7 ▲ Starting from the base of the
triangles, roll up to form spirals.

8 Place on the sheets and brush with
the remaining glaze. Sprinkle with
granulated sugar. Bake until golden,
15–20 minutes. Cool on a rack.

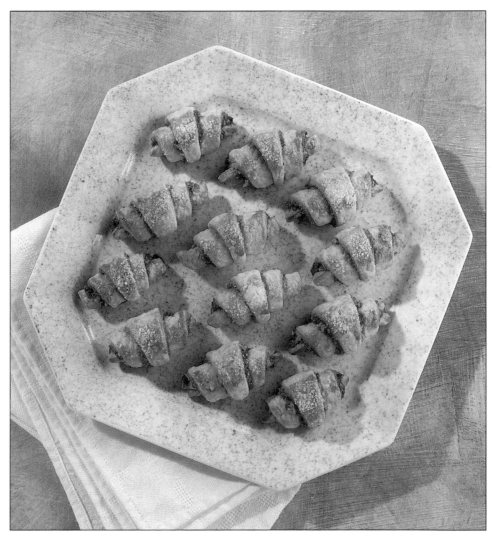

Chocolate Macaroons

MAKES 24

2 1-ounce squares unsweetened
   chocolate

1 cup blanched almonds

1 cup granulated sugar

⅓ cup egg whites (about 3 eggs)

½ teaspoon vanilla extract

¼ teaspoon almond extract

confectioners' sugar, for dusting

1 Preheat the oven to 325°F. Line 2 cookie sheets with wax paper and grease the paper.

2 ▼ Melt the chocolate in the top of a double boiler, or in a heatproof bowl set over a pan of hot water.

3 ▲ Grind the almonds finely in a food processor, blender, or nut grinder. Transfer to a mixing bowl.

4 ▲ Add the sugar, egg whites, vanilla, and almond extract and stir to blend. Stir in the chocolate. The mixture should just hold its shape. If it is too soft, refrigerate for 15 minutes.

5 ▲ Use a teaspoon and your hands to shape the dough into walnut-size balls. Place on the sheets and flatten slightly. Brush each ball with a little water and sift over a thin layer of confectioners' sugar. Bake until just firm, 10–12 minutes. With a metal spatula, transfer to a rack to cool.

~ **VARIATION** ~

For Chocolate Pine Nut Macaroons, spread ¾ cup pine nuts in a shallow dish. Press the balls of chocolate macaroon dough into the nuts to cover one side and bake as described, nut-side up.

Coconut Macaroons

MAKES 24

⅓ cup flour

⅛ teaspoon salt

2½ cups shredded coconut

⅔ cup sweetened condensed milk

1 teaspoon vanilla extract

1 Preheat the oven to 350°F. Grease 2 cookie sheets.

2 Sift the flour and salt into a bowl. Stir in the coconut.

3 ▲ Pour in the milk. Add the vanilla and stir from the center to make a very thick batter.

4 ▼ Drop heaped tablespoonfuls of batter 1 inch apart on prepared sheets. Bake until golden brown, about 20 minutes. Cool on a rack.

Chocolate Macaroons (top), Coconut Macaroons

Chocolate-Nut Refrigerator Cookies

MAKES 50

1 1-ounce square semisweet chocolate
1 1-ounce square unsweetened chocolate
2 cups flour
½ teaspoon salt
1 cup (2 sticks) unsalted butter, at room temperature
1 cup sugar
2 eggs
1 teaspoon vanilla extract
1 cup walnuts, finely chopped

1 Melt the chocolates in the top of a double boiler, or in a heatproof bowl set over a pan of gently simmering water. Set aside.

2 ▼ In a small bowl, sift together the flour and salt. Set aside.

3 With an electric mixer, cream the butter until soft. Add the sugar and continue beating until the mixture is light and fluffy.

4 Mix the eggs and vanilla, then gradually stir into the butter mixture.

5 ▲ Stir in the chocolate, then the flour. Stir in the nuts.

6 ▲ Divide the dough into 4 parts, and roll each into 2-inch diameter logs. Wrap tightly in foil and refrigerate or freeze until firm.

7 Preheat the oven to 375°F. Grease 2 cookie sheets.

8 With a sharp knife, cut the dough into ¼-inch slices. Place the rounds on the prepared sheets and bake until lightly colored, about 10 minutes. Transfer to a rack to cool.

~ VARIATION ~

For two-tone cookies, melt only 1 ounce of chocolate. Combine all the ingredients, except the chocolate, as above. Divide the dough in half. Add the chocolate to one half. Roll out the plain dough to a flat sheet. Roll out the chocolate dough, place on top of the plain dough and roll up. Wrap, slice and bake as described.

Cinnamon Refrigerator Cookies

MAKES 50

2⅛ cups flour

½ teaspoon salt

2 teaspoons ground cinnamon

1 cup (2 sticks) unsalted butter, at room temperature

1 cup sugar

2 eggs

1 teaspoon vanilla extract

1 In a bowl, sift together the flour, salt, and cinnamon. Set aside.

2 ▲ With an electric mixer, cream the butter until soft. Add the sugar and continue beating until the mixture is light and fluffy.

3 Beat the eggs and vanilla, then gradually stir into the butter mixture.

4 ▲ Stir in the dry ingredients.

5 ▲ Divide the dough into 4 parts, then roll each into 2-inch diameter logs. Wrap tightly in foil and refrigerate or freeze until firm.

6 Preheat the oven to 375°F. Grease 2 cookie sheets.

7 ▼ With a sharp knife, cut the dough into ¼-inch slices. Place the rounds on the prepared sheets and bake until lightly colored, about 10 minutes. With a metal spatula, transfer to a rack to cool.

Toasted Oat Meringues

MAKES 12

¾ cup old-fashioned oats

2 egg whites

⅛ teaspoon salt

1½ teaspoons cornstarch

¾ cup sugar

1 Preheat the oven to 275°F. Spread the oats in a baking tray and toast in the the oven until golden, about 10 minutes. Lower the heat to 250°F. Grease and flour a baking sheet.

~ **VARIATION** ~

Add ½ teaspoon ground cinnamon with the oats, and fold in gently.

2 ▼ With an electric mixer, beat the egg whites and salt until they start to form soft peaks.

3 Sift over the cornstarch and continue beating until the whites hold stiff peaks. Add half the sugar and whisk until glossy.

4 ▲ Add the remaining sugar and fold in, then fold in the oats.

5 Gently spoon the mixture onto the prepared sheet and bake for 2 hours.

6 When done, turn off the oven. Lift the meringues from the tray, turn over, and set in another place on the sheet to prevent sticking. Leave in the oven as it cools down.

Meringues

MAKES 24

4 egg whites

⅛ teaspoon salt

1¼ cups sugar

½ teaspoon vanilla or almond extract (optional)

1 cup whipped cream (optional)

1 Preheat the oven to 225°F. Grease and flour 2 large cookie sheets.

2 With an electric mixer, beat the egg whites and salt in a very clean metal bowl on low speed. When they start to form soft peaks, add half the sugar and continue beating until the mixture holds stiff peaks.

3 ▲ With a large metal spoon, fold in the remaining sugar and vanilla or almond extract, if using.

4 ▼ Pipe the meringue mixture or gently spoon it on the prepared sheet.

5 Bake for 2 hours. Turn off the oven. Loosen the meringues, invert, and set in another place on the sheets to prevent sticking. Leave in the oven as it cools. Serve sandwiched with whipped cream, if desired.

Toasted Oat Meringues (top), Meringues

Italian Almond Cookies

MAKES 48

1 cup unblanched almonds

1½ cups flour

½ cup sugar

⅛ teaspoon salt

⅛ teaspoon ground saffron

½ teaspoon baking soda

2 eggs

1 egg white, lightly beaten

~ COOK'S TIP ~

Serve these cookies after a meal, for dunking in glasses of sweet white wine, such as an Italian *Vin Santo* or a French *Muscat de Beaumes-de-Venise*.

---

1 Preheat the oven to 375°F. Grease and flour 2 cookie sheets.

2 ▲ Spread the almonds in a baking tray and bake until lightly browned, about 15 minutes. When cool, grind ¼ cup of the almonds in a food processor, blender, or nut grinder until pulverized. Coarsely chop the remaining almonds in 2 or 3 pieces each. Set aside.

3 ▲ Combine the flour, sugar, salt, saffron, baking soda, and ground almonds in a bowl and mix to blend. Make a well in the center and add the 2 eggs. Stir from the center to form a rough dough. Transfer to a floured surface and knead until well blended. Knead in the chopped almonds.

4 ▲ Divide the dough into 3 equal parts. With your hands, roll into logs about 1 inch in diameter. Place on one of the prepared sheets; leave room for spreading. Brush with the egg white. Bake for 20 minutes.

5 ▲ Remove from the oven and lower the heat to 275°F. With a very sharp knife, cut at an angle into ½-inch slices. Return the slices to the oven and bake for 25 minutes more. Transfer to a rack to cool.

Brandy Snaps

MAKES 18

4 tablespoons butter, at room temperature

²/₃ cup sugar

1 rounded tablespoon corn syrup

¹/₃ cup flour

¹/₂ teaspoon ground ginger

FOR THE FILLING

1 cup whipping cream

2 tablespoons brandy

1 With an electric mixer, cream together the butter and sugar until light and fluffy, then beat in the corn syrup. Sift over the flour and ginger and mix to a rough dough.

2 ▲ Transfer the dough to a work surface and knead until smooth. Cover and refrigerate for 30 minutes.

3 Preheat the oven to 375°F. Grease a cookie sheet.

4 ▲ Working in batches of 4, form walnut-size balls of dough. Place far apart on the prepared sheet and flatten slightly. Bake until golden and bubbling, about 10 minutes.

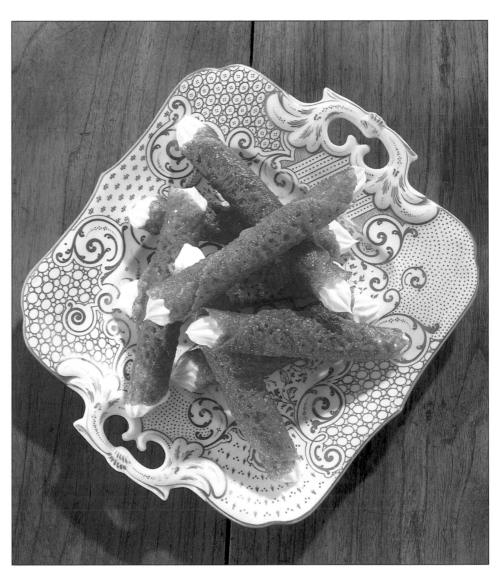

5 ▼ Remove from the oven and let cool a few moments. Working quickly, slide a metal spatula under each one, turn over, and wrap around the handle of a wooden spoon (have four spoons ready). If they firm up too quickly, reheat for a few seconds to soften. When firm, slide the snaps off and place on a rack to cool.

6 ▲ When all the brandy snaps are cool, prepare the filling. Whip the cream and brandy until soft peaks form. Fill a pastry bag with the brandy cream. Pipe into each end of the brandy snaps just before serving.

Hermits

MAKES 30

¾ cup flour

1½ teaspoons baking powder

1 teaspoon ground cinnamon

½ teaspoon grated nutmeg

¼ teaspoon ground cloves

¼ teaspoon ground allspice

1½ cup raisins

½ cup (1 stick) butter or margarine, at room temperature

½ cup sugar

2 eggs

½ cup molasses

½ cup walnuts, chopped

1 Preheat the oven to 350°F. Line the bottom and sides of a 13- × 9-inch pan with wax paper and grease.

2 Sift together the flour, baking powder, and spices.

3 ▲ Place the raisins in another bowl and toss with a few tablespoons of the flour mixture.

4 ▲ With an electric mixer, cream the butter or margarine and sugar together until light and fluffy. Beat in the eggs, 1 at a time, then the molasses. Stir in the flour mixture, raisins, and walnuts.

5 Spread evenly in the pan. Bake until just set, 15–18 minutes. Let cool in the pan before cutting into bars.

Butterscotch Meringue Bars

MAKES 12

4 tablespoons butter

1 cup dark brown sugar, firmly packed

1 egg

½ teaspoon vanilla extract

½ cup flour

½ teaspoon salt

¼ teaspoon grated nutmeg

FOR THE TOPPING

1 egg white

⅛ teaspoon salt

1 tablespoon light corn syrup

½ cup granulated sugar

½ cup walnuts, finely chopped

1 ▲ Combine the butter and brown sugar in a pan and cook until bubbling. Set aside to cool.

2 Preheat oven to 350°F. Line the bottom and sides of an 8-inch square cake pan with wax paper and grease.

3 Beat the egg and vanilla into cooled sugar mixture. Sift over the flour, salt, and nutmeg and fold in. Spread in the bottom of the pan.

4 ▲ For the topping, beat the egg white with the salt until it holds soft peaks. Beat in the corn syrup, then the sugar and continue beating until the mixture holds stiff peaks. Fold in the nuts and spread on top. Bake for 30 minutes. Cut into bars when cool.

Hermits (top), Butterscotch Meringue Bars

Chocolate Pecan Squares

MAKES 16

2 eggs

2 teaspoons vanilla extract

⅛ teaspoon salt

1½ cups pecans, coarsely chopped

½ cup flour

¼ cup sugar

½ cup dark corn syrup

3 1-ounce squares semisweet chocolate, finely chopped

3 tablespoons butter

16 pecan halves, for decorating

1 Preheat the oven to 325°F. Line the bottom and sides of an 8-inch square baking pan with wax paper and grease lightly.

2 ▼ Whisk together the eggs, vanilla, and salt. In another bowl, mix together the pecans and flour. Set both aside.

3 In a saucepan, bring the sugar and corn syrup to a boil. Remove from the heat and stir in the chocolate and butter to blend thoroughly with a wooden spoon.

4 ▲ Mix in the beaten eggs, then fold in the pecan mixture.

5 Pour the batter into the prepared pan and bake until set, about 35 minutes. Cool in the pan for 10 minutes before unmolding. Cut into 2-inch squares and press pecan halves into the tops while warm. Cool completely on a rack.

Raisin Brownies

MAKES 16

½ cup (1 stick) butter or margarine

½ cup unsweetened cocoa powder

2 eggs

1 cup sugar

1 teaspoon vanilla extract

⅓ cup flour

¾ cup walnuts, chopped

½ cup raisins

1 Preheat the oven to 350°F. Line the bottom and sides of an 8-inch square baking pan and grease.

2 ▼ Gently melt the butter or margarine in a small saucepan. Remove from the heat and stir in the cocoa powder.

3 With an electric mixer, beat the eggs, sugar, and vanilla together until light. Add the cocoa mixture and stir to blend.

4 ▲ Sift the flour over the cocoa mixture and gently fold in. Add the walnuts and raisins and scrape the batter into the prepared pan.

5 Bake in the center of the oven for 30 minutes. Do not overbake. Leave in the pan to cool before cutting into 2-inch squares and removing. The brownies should be soft and moist.

Chocolate Pecan Squares (top), Raisin Brownies

Apricot Bars

MAKES 12

½ cup light brown sugar, firmly packed

¾ cup flour

6 tablespoons cold unsalted butter, cut in pieces

FOR THE TOPPING

1 cup dried apricots

1 cup water

grated rind of 1 lemon

⅓ cup granulated sugar

2 teaspoons cornstarch

½ cup walnuts, chopped

1 Preheat the oven to 350°F.

2 ▲ In a bowl, combine the brown sugar and flour. With a pastry blender, cut in the butter until the mixture resembles coarse crumbs.

3 ▲ Transfer to an 8-inch square baking pan and press into an even layer. Bake for 15 minutes. Remove from the oven but leave the oven on.

4 Meanwhile, for the topping, combine the apricots and water in a saucepan and simmer until soft, about 10 minutes. Strain the liquid and reserve. Chop the apricots.

5 ▲ Return the apricots to the saucepan and add the lemon rind, granulated sugar, cornstarch, and 4 tablespoons of the soaking liquid. Cook for 1 minute.

6 ▲ Cool slightly before spreading the topping over the base. Sprinkle over the walnuts and continue baking for 20 minutes more. Let cool in the pan before cutting into bars.

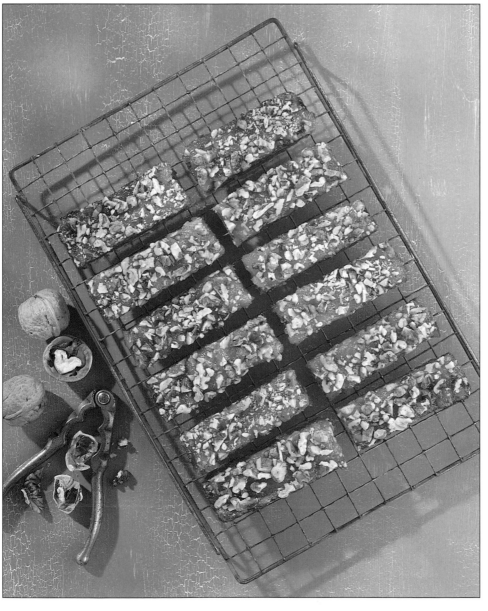

Marbled Brownies

MAKES 24

8 1-ounce squares semisweet chocolate
6 tablespoons butter
4 eggs
1½ cups sugar
1 cup flour
½ teaspoon salt
1 teaspoon baking powder
2 teaspoons vanilla extract
l cup walnuts, chopped
FOR THE PLAIN BATTER
4 tablespoons butter, at room temperature
6 ounces cream cheese
½ cup sugar
2 eggs
2 tablespoons flour
1 teaspoon vanilla extract

1 Preheat the oven to 350°F. Line the bottom and sides of a 13- × 9-inch pan with wax paper and grease.

2 Melt the chocolate and butter over very low heat, stirring constantly. Set aside to cool.

3 Meanwhile, beat the eggs until light and fluffy. Gradually add the sugar and continue beating until blended. Sift over the flour, salt, and baking powder and fold to combine.

4 ▲ Stir in the cooled chocolate mixture. Add the vanilla and walnuts. Measure and set aside 2 cups of the chocolate batter.

5 ▲ For the plain batter, cream the butter and cream cheese with an electric mixer.

6 Add the sugar and continue beating until blended. Beat in the eggs, flour, and vanilla.

7 Spread the unmeasured chocolate batter in pan. Pour over the cream cheese mixture. Drop spoonfuls of the reserved chocolate batter on top.

8 ▲ With a metal spatula, swirl the mixtures to marble. Do not blend completely. Bake until just set, 35–40 minutes. Unmold when cool and cut into squares for serving.

Fig Bars

MAKES 48

2 cups dried figs

3 eggs

¾ cup granulated sugar

¾ cup flour

1 teaspoon baking powder

½ teaspoon ground cinnamon

¼ teaspoon ground cloves

¼ teaspoon grated nutmeg

¼ teaspoon salt

¾ cup walnuts, finely chopped

2 tablespoons brandy or cognac

confectioners' sugar, for dusting

1 Preheat the oven to 325°F. Line a 12- × 8- × 1½-inch pan with wax paper and grease.

2 ▲ With a sharp knife, chop the figs roughly. Set aside.

3 In a bowl, whisk the eggs and sugar until well blended. In another bowl, sift together the dry ingredients, then fold into the egg mixture in several batches.

4 ▼ Stir in the figs, walnuts, and brandy or cognac.

5 Scrape the mixture into the prepared pan and bake until the top is firm and brown, 35–40 minutes. It should still be soft underneath.

6 Let cool in the pan for 5 minutes, then unmold and transfer to a sheet of wax paper lightly sprinkled with confectioners' sugar. Cut into bars.

Lemon Bars

MAKES 36

½ cup confectioners' sugar

1½ cups flour

½ teaspoon salt

¾ cup (1½ sticks) butter, cut in small pieces

FOR THE TOPPING

4 eggs

1½ cups granulated sugar

grated rind of 1 lemon

½ cup fresh lemon juice

¾ cup whipping cream

confectioners' sugar, for dusting

1 Preheat the oven to 325°F. Grease a 13- × 9-inch baking pan.

2 Sift the sugar, flour, and salt into a bowl. With a pastry blender, cut in the butter until the mixture resembles coarse crumbs.

3 ▲ Press the mixture into the bottom of the prepared pan. Bake until golden brown, about 20 minutes.

4 Meanwhile, for the topping, whisk the eggs and sugar together until blended. Add the lemon rind and juice and mix well.

5 ▲ Lightly whip the cream and fold into the egg mixture. Pour over the still warm crust, return to the oven, and bake until set, about 40 minutes.

6 Cool completely before cutting into bars. Dust with confectioners' sugar.

Fig Bars (top), Lemon Bars

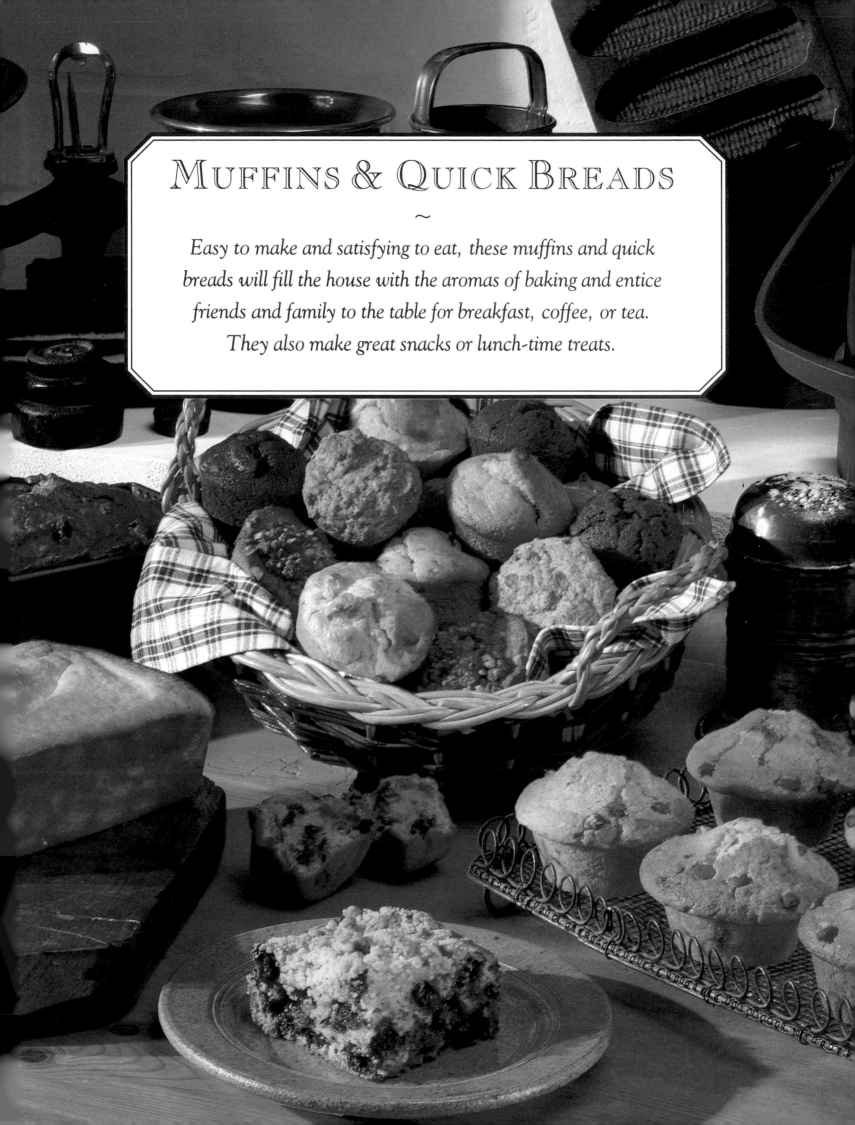

MUFFINS & QUICK BREADS

~

Easy to make and satisfying to eat, these muffins and quick breads will fill the house with the aromas of baking and entice friends and family to the table for breakfast, coffee, or tea. They also make great snacks or lunch-time treats.

Chocolate Chip Muffins

MAKES 10

½ cup (1 stick) butter or margarine, at room temperature

⅓ cup granulated sugar

2 tablespoons dark brown sugar

2 eggs, at room temperature

1½ cups cake flour

1 teaspoon baking powder

½ cup milk

1 cup semisweet chocolate chips

1 Preheat the oven to 375°F. Grease 10 muffin cups or use paper liners.

2 ▼ With an electric mixer, cream the butter or margarine until soft. Add both sugars and beat until light and fluffy. Beat in the eggs, 1 at a time.

3 Sift together the flour and baking powder, twice. Fold into the butter mixture, alternating with the milk.

4 ▲ Divide half the mixture between the muffin cups. Sprinkle several chocolate chips on top, then cover with a spoonful of the batter. To ensure even baking, half-fill any empty cups with water.

5 Bake until lightly colored, about 25 minutes. Let stand 5 minutes before unmolding.

Chocolate Walnut Muffins

MAKES 12

¾ cup (1½ sticks) unsalted butter

4 1-ounce squares semisweet chocolate

1 1-ounce square unsweetened chocolate

1 cup granulated sugar

¼ cup dark brown sugar, firmly packed

4 eggs

1 teaspoon vanilla extract

¼ teaspoon almond extract

¾ cup flour

1 cup walnuts, chopped

1 Preheat the oven to 350°F. Grease a 12-cup muffin pan or use paper liners.

2 ▼ Melt the butter with the two chocolates in the top of a double boiler or in a heatproof bowl set over a pan of hot water. Transfer to a large mixing bowl.

3 Stir both the sugars into the chocolate mixture. Mix in the eggs, 1 at a time, then add the vanilla and almond extracts.

4 Sift over the flour and fold in.

5 ▲ Stir in the walnuts.

6 Fill the prepared cups almost to the top and bake until a cake tester inserted in the center barely comes out clean, 30–35 minutes. Let stand 5 minutes before transferring to a rack to cool completely.

Chocolate Chip Muffins (top), Chocolate Walnut Muffins

Raisin Bran Muffins

MAKES 15

4 tablespoons butter or margarine
⅔ cup all-purpose flour
½ cup whole-wheat flour
1½ teaspoons baking soda
⅛ teaspoon salt
1 teaspoon ground cinnamon
½ cup bran
½ cup raisins
⅓ cup dark brown sugar, firmly packed
¼ cup granulated sugar
1 egg
1 cup buttermilk
juice of ½ lemon

1 Preheat the oven to 400°F. Grease 15 muffin cups or use paper liners.

2 ▲ Place the butter or margarine in a saucepan and melt over gentle heat. Set aside.

3 In a mixing bowl, sift together the all-purpose flour, whole-wheat flour, baking soda, salt, and cinnamon.

4 ▲ Add the bran, raisins, and sugars and stir until blended.

5 In another bowl, mix together the egg, buttermilk, lemon juice, and melted butter.

6 ▲ Add the buttermilk mixture to the dry ingredients and stir lightly and quickly just until moistened; do not mix until smooth.

7 ▲ Spoon the batter into the prepared muffin cups, filling them almost to the top. Half-fill any empty cups with water.

8 Bake until golden, 15–20 minutes. Serve warm or at room temperature.

Raspberry Crumble Muffins

MAKES 12

1½ cups flour
¼ cup granulated sugar
¼ cup light brown sugar, firmly packed
2 teaspoons baking powder
⅛ teaspoon salt
1 teaspoon ground cinnamon
½ cup (1 stick) butter, melted
1 egg
½ cup milk
1¼ cups fresh raspberries
grated rind of 1 lemon
FOR THE CRUMBLE TOPPING
¼ cup pecans, finely chopped
¼ cup dark brown sugar, firmly packed
3 tablespoons flour
1 teaspoon ground cinnamon
3 tablespoons butter, melted

1 Preheat the oven to 350°F. Grease a 12-cup muffin pan or use paper liners.

2 Sift the flour into a bowl. Add the sugars, baking powder, salt, and cinnamon and stir to blend.

3 ▲ Make a well in the center. Place the butter, egg, and milk in the well and mix until just combined. Stir in the raspberries and lemon rind. Spoon the batter into the prepared muffin cups, filling them almost to the top.

4 ▼ For the crumble topping, mix the pecans, dark brown sugar, flour, and cinnamon in a bowl. Add the melted butter and stir to blend.

5 ▲ Spoon some of the crumble over each muffin. Bake until browned, about 25 minutes. Transfer to a rack to cool slightly. Serve warm.

Carrot Muffins

MAKES 12

¾ cup margarine, at room temperature

½ cup dark brown sugar, firmly packed

1 egg, at room temperature

1 tablespoon water

2 cups grated carrots

1¼ cups flour

1 teaspoon baking powder

½ teaspoon baking soda

1 teaspoon ground cinnamon

¼ teaspoon grated nutmeg

½ teaspoon salt

1 Preheat the oven to 350°F. Grease a 12-cup muffin pan or use paper liners.

2 With an electric mixer, cream the margarine and sugar until light and fluffy. Beat in the egg and water.

3 ▲ Stir in the carrots.

4 Sift over the flour, baking powder, baking soda, cinnamon, nutmeg, and salt. Stir to blend.

5 ▼ Spoon the batter into the prepared muffin cups, filling them almost to the top. Bake until the tops spring back when touched lightly, about 35 minutes. Let stand 10 minutes before transferring to a rack.

Dried Cherry Muffins

MAKES 16

1 cup plain yogurt

1 cup dried cherries

½ cup (1 stick) butter, at room temperature

¾ cup sugar

2 eggs, at room temperature

1 teaspoon vanilla extract

1¾ cups flour

2 teaspoons baking powder

1 teaspoon baking soda

⅛ teaspoon salt

1 In a mixing bowl, combine the yogurt and cherries. Cover and let stand for 30 minutes.

2 Preheat the oven to 350°F. Grease 16 muffin cups or use paper liners.

3 With an electric mixer, cream the butter and sugar together until light and fluffy.

4 ▼ Add the eggs, 1 at a time, beating well after each addition. Add the vanilla and the cherry mixture and stir to blend. Set aside.

5 ▲ In another bowl, sift together the flour, baking powder, baking soda, and salt. Fold into the cherry mixture in 3 batches; do not overmix.

6 Fill the prepared cups two-thirds full. For even baking, half-fill any empty cups with water. Bake until the tops spring back when touched lightly, about 20 minutes. Transfer to a rack to cool.

Carrot Muffins (top), Dried Cherry Muffins

Glazed Banana Spice Loaf

MAKES 1 LOAF

1 large ripe banana

½ cup (1 stick) butter, at room temperature

¾ cup granulated sugar

2 eggs, at room temperature

1½ cups flour

1 teaspoon salt

1 teaspoon baking soda

½ teaspoon grated nutmeg

¼ teaspoon ground allspice

¼ teaspoon ground cloves

¾ cup sour cream

1 teaspoon vanilla extract

FOR THE GLAZE

1 cup confectioners' sugar

1–2 tablespoons fresh lemon juice

1 Preheat the oven to 350°F. Line an 8½- × 4½-inch loaf pan with wax paper and grease.

2 ▼ With a fork, mash the banana in a bowl. Set aside.

3 With an electric mixer, cream the butter and sugar until light and fluffy. Add the eggs, 1 at a time, beating to blend well after each addition.

4 Sift together the flour, salt, baking soda, nutmeg, allspice, and cloves. Add to the butter mixture and stir to combine well.

5 ▲ Add the sour cream, banana, and vanilla and mix just enough to blend. Pour into the prepared pan.

6 ▲ Bake until the top springs back when touched lightly, 45–50 minutes. Let cool in the pan for 10 minutes before unmolding.

7 ▲ For the glaze, combine the confectioners' sugar and lemon juice, then stir until smooth.

8 To glaze, place the cooled loaf on a rack set over a baking sheet. Pour the glaze over the top of the bread and allow to set.

Date-Nut Bread

MAKES 1 LOAF

1 cup pitted dates, chopped
¾ cup boiling water
4 tablespoons unsalted butter, at room temperature
¼ cup dark brown sugar, firmly packed
¼ cup granulated sugar
1 egg, at room temperature
2 tablespoons brandy
1⅓ cups flour
2 teaspoons baking powder
½ teaspoon salt
¾ teaspoon freshly grated nutmeg
¾ cup pecans, coarsely chopped

1 ▲ Place the dates in a bowl and pour over the boiling water. Set aside to cool.

2 Preheat the oven to 350°F. Line the bottom and sides of a 9- × 5-inch loaf pan with wax paper and grease.

3 ▲ With an electric mixer, cream the butter and sugars until light and fluffy. Beat in the egg and brandy, then set aside.

4 Sift the flour, baking powder, salt, and nutmeg together, 3 times.

5 ▼ Fold the dry ingredients into the sugar mixture in 3 batches, alternating with the dates and water.

6 ▲ Fold in the pecans.

7 Pour the batter into the prepared pan and bake until a cake tester inserted in the center comes out clean, 45–50 minutes. Let cool in the pan for 10 minutes before transferring to a rack to cool completely.

Orange Honey Bread

MAKES 1 LOAF

2½ cups flour

2½ teaspoons baking powder

½ teaspoon baking soda

½ teaspoon salt

2 tablespoons margarine

1 cup thin honey

1 egg, at room temperature, lightly beaten

1½ tablespoons grated orange rind

¾ cup freshly squeezed orange juice

¾ cup walnuts, chopped

1 Preheat the oven to 325°F.

2 Sift together the flour, baking powder, baking soda, and salt.

3 Line the bottom and sides of a 9- × 5-inch loaf pan with wax paper and grease.

4 ▲ With an electric mixer, cream the margarine until soft. Stir in the honey until blended, then stir in the egg. Add the orange rind and stir to combine thoroughly.

5 ▲ Fold the flour mixture into the honey and egg mixture in 3 batches, alternating with the orange juice. Stir in the walnuts.

6 Pour into the pan and bake until a cake tester inserted in the center comes out clean, 60–70 minutes. Let stand 10 minutes before unmolding onto a rack to cool.

Applesauce Bread

MAKES 1 LOAF

1 egg

1 cup applesauce

4 tablespoons butter or margarine, melted

½ cup dark brown sugar, firmly packed

¼ cup granulated sugar

2 cups flour

2 teaspoons baking powder

½ teaspoon baking soda

½ teaspoon salt

1 teaspoon ground cinnamon

½ teaspoon grated nutmeg

½ cup currants or raisins

½ cup pecans, chopped

1 Preheat the oven to 350°F. Line the bottom and sides of a 9- × 5-inch loaf pan with wax paper and grease.

2 ▲ Break the egg into a bowl and beat lightly. Stir in the applesauce, butter or margarine, and both sugars. Set aside.

3 In another bowl, sift together the flour, baking powder, baking soda, salt, cinnamon, and nutmeg. Fold dry ingredients into the applesauce mixture in 3 batches.

4 ▼ Stir in the currants or raisins, and pecans.

5 Pour into the prepared pan and bake until a cake tester inserted in the center comes out clean, about 1 hour. Let stand 10 minutes before unmolding and transferring to a cooling rack.

Orange Honey Bread (top), Applesauce Bread

Blueberry Streusel Bread

MAKES 8 PIECES

4 tablespoons butter or margarine, at room temperature

¾ cup sugar

1 egg, at room temperature

½ cup milk

2 cups flour

2 teaspoons baking powder

½ teaspoon salt

2 cups fresh blueberries

FOR THE TOPPING

½ cup sugar

⅓ cup flour

½ teaspoon ground cinnamon

4 tablespoons butter, cut in pieces

1 Preheat the oven to 375°F. Grease a 9-inch square baking dish.

2 With an electric mixer, cream the butter or margarine with the sugar until light and fluffy. Add the egg, beat to combine, then mix in the milk until blended.

3 ▼ Sift over the flour, baking powder, and salt and stir just enough to blend the ingredients.

4 ▲ Add the blueberries and stir.

5 Transfer to the baking dish.

6 ▲ For the topping, place the sugar, flour, cinnamon, and butter in a mixing bowl. Cut in with a pastry blender until the mixture resembles coarse crumbs.

7 ▲ Sprinkle the topping over the batter in the pan.

8 Bake until a cake tester inserted in the center comes out clean, about 45 minutes. Serve warm or cold.

Sweet Sesame Loaf

MAKES 1 OR 2 LOAVES

⅔ cup sesame seeds

2 cups flour

2½ teaspoons baking powder

1 teaspoon salt

4 tablespoons butter or margarine, at
   room temperature

⅔ cup sugar

2 eggs, at room temperature

grated rind of 1 lemon

1½ cups milk

1 Preheat the oven to 350°F. Line a
10- × 6-inch baking pan, or 2 small
loaf pans, with wax paper and grease.

2 ▲ Reserve 2 tablespoons of the
sesame seeds. Spread the rest on a
baking sheet and bake until lightly
toasted, about 10 minutes.

3 Sift the flour, salt, and baking
powder into a bowl.

4 ▲ Stir in the toasted sesame seeds
and set aside.

5 With an electric mixer, cream the
butter or margarine and sugar together
until light and fluffy. Beat in the eggs,
then stir in the lemon rind and milk.

6 ▼ Pour the milk mixture over the
dry ingredients and fold in with a large
metal spoon until just blended.

7 ▲ Pour into the pan and sprinkle
over the reserved sesame seeds.

8 Bake until a cake tester inserted in
the center comes out clean, about 1
hour. Let cool in the pan for 10
minutes before unmolding.

Corn Bread

MAKES 1 LOAF

1 cup flour
1/3 cup sugar
1 teaspoon salt
1 tablespoon baking powder
1½ cups cornmeal
1½ cups milk
2 eggs
6 tablespoons butter, melted
8 tablespoons margarine, melted

1 Preheat the oven to 400°F. Line the bottom and sides of a 9- × 5-inch loaf pan with wax paper and grease.

2 Sift the flour, sugar, salt, and baking powder into a mixing bowl.

3 ▼ Add the cornmeal and stir to blend. Make a well in the center.

4 ▲ Whisk together the milk, eggs, butter, and margarine. Pour the mixture into the well. Stir until just blended; do not overmix.

5 Pour into the pan and bake until a cake tester inserted in the center comes out clean, about 45 minutes. Serve hot or at room temperature.

Tex-Mex Corn Bread

MAKES 9 SQUARES

3–4 whole canned chile peppers, drained
2 eggs
2 cups buttermilk
4 tablespoons butter, melted
½ cup flour
1 teaspoon baking soda
2 teaspoons salt
1½ cups cornmeal
2 cups corn kernels

1 Preheat the oven to 400°F. Line the bottom and sides of a 9-inch square cake pan with wax paper and grease lightly.

2 ▲ With a sharp knife, chop the chiles in a fine dice and set aside.

3 ▲ In a large bowl, whisk the eggs until frothy, then whisk in the buttermilk. Add the melted butter.

4 In another large bowl, sift together the flour, baking soda, and salt. Fold into the buttermilk mixture in 3 batches, then fold in the cornmeal in 3 batches.

5 ▲ Fold in the chiles and corn.

6 Pour the batter into the prepared pan and bake until a cake tester inserted in the middle comes out clean, 25–30 minutes. Let stand for 2–3 minutes before unmolding. Cut into squares and serve warm.

Corn Bread (top), Tex-Mex Corn Bread

Whole-Wheat Scones

MAKES 16

¾ cup (1½ sticks) cold butter

2 cups whole-wheat flour

1 cup all-purpose flour

2 tablespoons sugar

½ teaspoon salt

2½ teaspoons baking soda

2 eggs

¾ cup buttermilk

¼ cup raisins

1 Preheat the oven to 400°F. Grease and flour a large baking sheet.

2 ▲ Cut the butter into small pieces.

3 Combine the dry ingredients in a bowl. Add the butter and cut in with a pastry blender until the mixture resembles coarse crumbs. Set aside.

4 In another bowl, whisk together the eggs and buttermilk. Set aside 2 tablespoons for glazing.

5 Stir the remaining egg mixture into the dry ingredients until it just holds together. Stir in the raisins.

6 Roll out the dough about ¾ inch thick. Stamp out circles with a cookie cutter. Place on the prepared sheet and brush with the glaze.

7 Bake until golden, 12–15 minutes. Allow to cool slightly before serving. Split in two with a fork while still warm and spread with butter and jam, if wished.

Orange Raisin Scones

MAKES 16

2 cups flour

1½ tablespoons baking powder

⅓ cup sugar

½ teaspoon salt

5 tablespoons butter, diced

5 tablespoons margarine, diced

grated rind of 1 large orange

⅓ cup raisins

½ cup buttermilk

milk, for glazing

1 Preheat the oven to 425°F. Grease and flour a large baking sheet.

2 Combine the dry ingredients in a large bowl. Add the butter and margarine and cut in with a pastry blender until the mixture resembles coarse crumbs.

3 ▲ Add the orange rind and raisins.

4 Gradually stir in the buttermilk to form a soft dough.

5 ▲ Roll out the dough about ¾ inch thick. Stamp out circles with a cookie cutter.

6 ▲ Place on the prepared sheet and brush the tops with milk.

7 Bake until golden, 12–15 minutes. Serve hot or warm, with butter or whipped cream, and jam.

~ COOK'S TIP ~

For light tender scones, handle the dough as little as possible. If you wish, split the scones when cool and toast them under a preheated broiler. Butter them while still hot.

Whole-Wheat Scones (top), Orange Raisin Scones

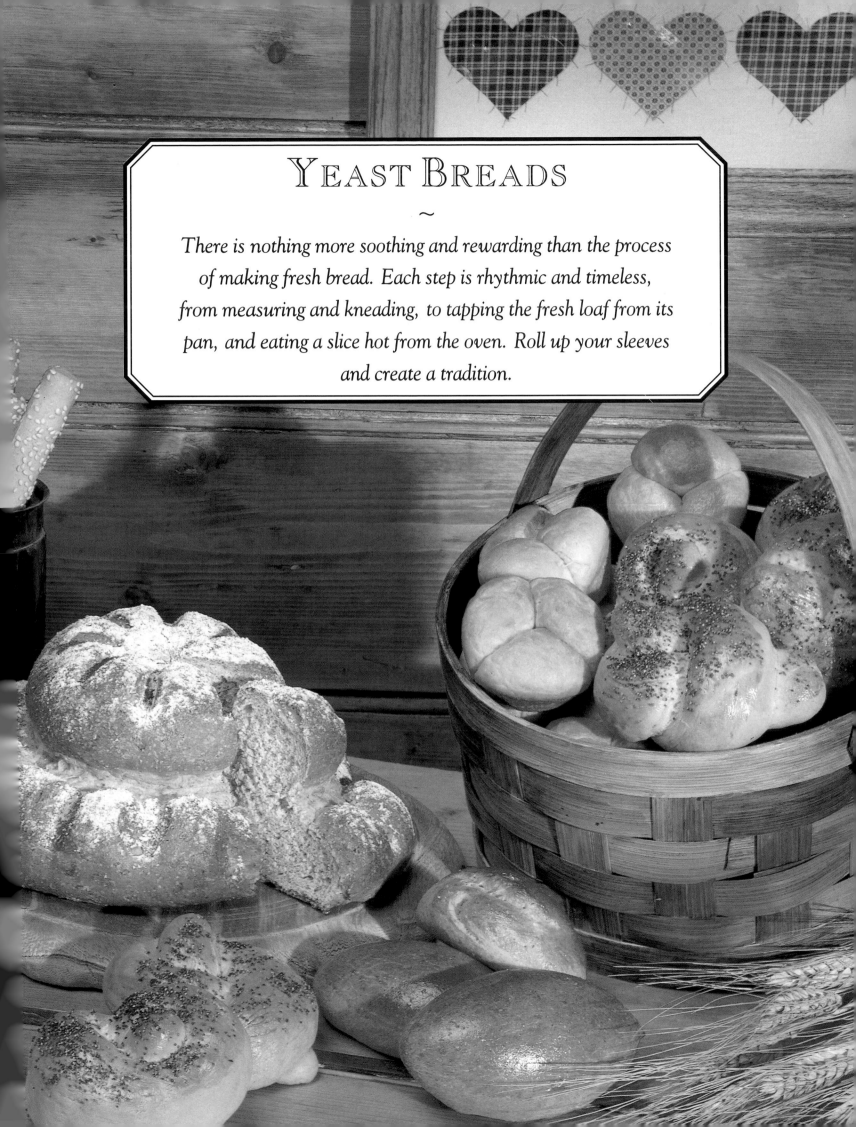

YEAST BREADS

~

There is nothing more soothing and rewarding than the process of making fresh bread. Each step is rhythmic and timeless, from measuring and kneading, to tapping the fresh loaf from its pan, and eating a slice hot from the oven. Roll up your sleeves and create a tradition.

White Bread

MAKES 2 LOAVES

¼ cup lukewarm water
1 package active dry yeast
2 tablespoons sugar
2 cups lukewarm milk
2 tablespoons butter or margarine, at room temperature
2 teaspoons salt
6–6½ cups flour

1 Combine the water, yeast, and 1 tablespoon of sugar in a measuring cup and let stand 15 minutes until the mixture is frothy.

2 ▼ Pour the milk into a large bowl. Add the remaining sugar, the butter or margarine, and salt. Stir in the yeast mixture.

3 Stir in the flour, 1 cup at a time, until a stiff dough is obtained. Alternatively, use a food processor.

4 ▲ Transfer the dough to a floured surface. To knead, push the dough away from you with the palm of your hand, then fold it toward you, and push it away again. Repeat until the dough is smooth and elastic.

5 Place the dough in a large greased bowl, cover with a plastic bag, and leave to rise in a warm place until doubled in volume, 2–3 hours.

6 Grease 2 9- × 5-inch loaf pans.

7 ▲ Punch down the risen dough with your fist and divide in half. Form into loaf shapes and place in the pans, seam-side down. Cover and let rise in a warm place until almost doubled in volume, about 45 minutes.

8 Preheat the oven to 375°F.

9 Bake until firm and brown, 45–50 minutes. Unmold and tap the bottom of a loaf: if it sounds hollow the loaf is done. If necessary, return to the oven and bake a few minutes more.

10 Let cool on a rack.

Country Bread

MAKES 2 LOAVES

2½ cups whole-wheat flour
2½ cups all-purpose flour
1 cup strong flour
4 teaspoons salt
4 tablespoons butter, at room temperature
2 cups lukewarm milk
FOR THE STARTER
1 package active dry yeast
1 cup lukewarm water
1 cup all-purpose flour
¼ teaspoon sugar

1 ▲ For the starter, combine the yeast, water, flour, and sugar in a bowl and stir with a fork. Cover and leave in a warm place for 2–3 hours, or leave overnight in a cool place.

2 Place the flours, salt, and butter in a food processor and process just until blended, 1–2 minutes.

3 Stir together the milk and starter, then slowly pour into the processor, with the motor running, until the mixture forms a dough. If necessary, add more water. Alternatively, the dough can be mixed by hand. Transfer to a floured surface and knead until smooth and elastic.

4 Place in an ungreased bowl, cover with a plastic bag, and leave to rise in a warm place until doubled in volume, about 1½ hours.

5 Transfer to a floured surface and knead briefly. Return to the bowl and leave to rise until tripled in volume, about 1½ hours.

6 ▲ Divide the dough in half. Cut off one-third of the dough from each half and shape into balls. Shape the larger remaining portion of each half into balls. Grease a baking sheet.

7 ▲ For each loaf, top the large ball with the small ball and press the center with the handle of a wooden spoon to secure. Cover with a plastic bag, slash the top, and leave to rise.

8 Preheat the oven to 400°F. Dust the dough with whole-wheat flour and bake until the top is browned and the bottom sounds hollow when tapped, 45–50 minutes. Cool on a rack.

Braided Loaf

MAKES 1 LOAF

1 package active dry yeast

1 teaspoon honey

1 cup lukewarm milk

4 tablespoons butter, melted

3 cups flour

1 teaspoon salt

1 egg, lightly beaten

1 egg yolk beaten with 1 teaspoon milk,
  for glazing

1 ▼ Combine the yeast, honey, milk, and butter, stir, and leave for 15 minutes to dissolve.

2 In a large bowl, mix together the flour and salt. Make a well in the center and add the yeast mixture and egg. With a wooden spoon, stir from the center, incorporating flour with each turn, to obtain a rough dough.

3 Transfer to a floured surface and knead until smooth and elastic. Place in a clean bowl, cover, and leave to rise in a warm place until doubled in volume, about 1½ hours.

4 Grease a baking sheet. Punch down the dough and divide into three equal pieces. Roll to shape each piece into a long thin strip.

5 ▲ Begin braiding from the center strip, tucking in the ends. Cover loosely and leave to rise in a warm place for 30 minutes.

6 ▲ Preheat the oven to 375°F. Place the bread in a cool place while oven heats. Brush with the glaze and bake until golden, 40–45 minutes. Set on a rack to cool completely.

Oatmeal Bread

MAKES 2 LOAVES

| 2 cups milk |
| 2 tablespoons butter |
| ¼ cup dark brown sugar, firmly packed |
| 2 teaspoons salt |
| 1 package active dry yeast |
| ¼ cup lukewarm water |
| 2½ cups rolled oats (not quick-cooking) |
| 5–6 cups flour |

1 ▲ Scald the milk. Remove from the heat and stir in the butter, brown sugar and salt. Leave until lukewarm.

2 Combine the yeast and warm water in a large bowl and leave until the yeast is dissolved and the mixture is frothy. Stir in the milk mixture.

3 ▲ Add 2 cups of the oats and enough flour to obtain a soft dough.

4 Transfer to a floured surface and knead until smooth and elastic.

5 ▲ Place in a greased bowl, cover with a plastic bag, and leave until doubled in volume, 2–3 hours.

6 Grease a large baking sheet. Transfer the dough to a lightly floured surface and divide in half.

7 ▼ Shape into rounds. Place on the baking sheet, cover with a dish towel, and leave to rise until doubled in volume, about 1 hour.

8 Preheat the oven to 400°F. Score the tops and sprinkle with the remaining oats. Bake until the bottoms sound hollow when tapped, 45–50 minutes. Cool on racks.

Potato Bread

MAKES 2 LOAVES

4 teaspoons active dry yeast

1 cup lukewarm milk

½ pound potatoes, boiled (reserve 1 cup of potato cooking liquid)

2 tablespoons oil

4 teaspoons salt

6–6½ cups flour

1 Combine the yeast and milk in a large bowl and leave to dissolve, about 15 minutes.

2 Meanwhile, mash the potatoes.

3 ▲ Add the potatoes, oil, and salt to the yeast mixture and mix well. Stir in 1 cup of the cooking water, then stir in the flour, 1 cup at a time, to form a stiff dough.

4 Transfer to a floured surface and knead until smooth and elastic. Return to the bowl, cover, and leave in a warm place until doubled in size, 1–1½ hours. Punch down, then leave to rise for another 40 minutes.

5 Grease 2 9- × 5-inch loaf pans. Roll the dough into 20 small balls. Place two rows of balls in each pan. Leave until the dough has risen above the rim of the pans.

6 Preheat the oven to 400°F. Bake for 10 minutes, then lower the heat to 375°F and bake until the bottoms sound hollow when tapped, about 40 minutes. Cool on a rack.

Irish Soda Bread

MAKES 1 LOAF

2 cups all-purpose flour

1 cup whole-wheat flour

1 teaspoon baking soda

1 teaspoon salt

2 tablespoons butter or margarine, at room temperature

1¼ cups buttermilk

1 tablespoon all-purpose flour, for dusting

1 Preheat the oven to 400°F. Grease a baking sheet.

2 Sift the flours, baking soda, and salt together into a bowl. Make a well in the center and add the butter or margarine and buttermilk. Working outward from the center, stir with a fork until a soft dough is formed.

3 ▲ With floured hands, gather the dough into a ball.

4 ▲ Transfer to a floured surface and knead for 3 minutes. Shape the dough into a large round.

5 ▲ Place on the baking sheet. Cut a cross in the top with a sharp knife.

6 ▲ Dust with flour. Bake until brown, 40–50 minutes. Transfer to a rack to cool.

Potato Bread (top), Irish Soda Bread

Dill Bread

MAKES 2 LOAVES

4 teaspoons active dry yeast
2 cups lukewarm water
2 tablespoons sugar
7½ cups flour
½ onion, chopped
4 tablespoons oil
l large bunch of dill, finely chopped
2 eggs, lightly beaten
½ cup cottage cheese
4 teaspoons salt
milk, for glazing

1 Mix together the yeast, water, and sugar in a large bowl and leave for 15 minutes to dissolve.

2 ▼ Stir in 3 cups of the flour. Cover and leave to rise in a warm place for 45 minutes.

3 ▲ In a skillet, cook the onion in 1 tablespoon of the oil until soft. Set aside to cool, then stir into the yeast mixture. Stir the dill, eggs, cottage cheese, salt, and remaining oil into the yeast mixture. Gradually add the remaining flour until too stiff to stir.

4 ▲ Transfer to a floured surface and knead until smooth and elastic. Place in a bowl, cover, and leave to rise until doubled in volume, 1–1½ hours.

5 ▲ Grease a large baking sheet. Cut the dough in half and shape into 2 rounds. Leave to rise in a warm place for 30 minutes.

6 Preheat the oven to 375°F. Score the tops, brush with the milk, and bake until browned, about 50 minutes. Cool on a rack.

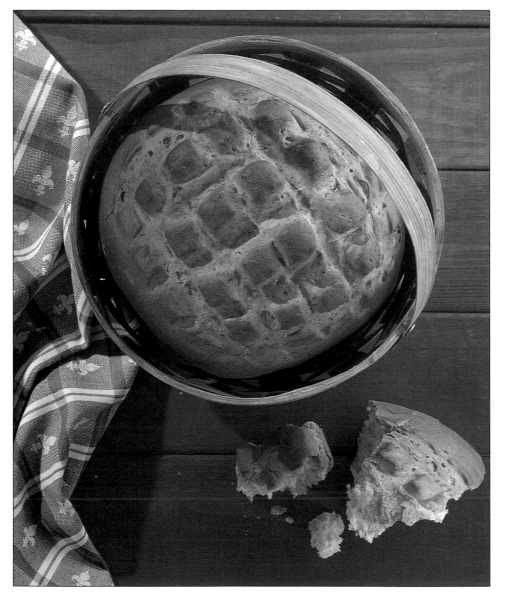

Pecan Rye Bread

MAKES 2 LOAVES

1½ packages active dry yeast
3 cups lukewarm water
5 cups all-purpose flour
3 cups rye flour
2 tablespoons salt
1 tablespoon honey
2 teaspoons caraway seeds, (optional)
½ cup (1 stick) butter, at room temperature
2 cups pecans, chopped

1 Combine the yeast and ½ cup of the water. Stir and leave for 15 minutes to dissolve.

2 In the bowl of an electric mixer, combine the flours, salt, honey, caraway seeds, and butter. With the dough hook, mix on low speed until well blended.

3 Add the yeast mixture and the remaining water and mix on medium speed until the dough forms a ball.

4 ▲ Transfer to a floured surface and knead in the pecans.

5 Return the dough to a clean bowl, cover with a plastic bag, and leave in a warm place until doubled in volume, about 2 hours.

6 Grease 2 8½- × 4½-inch bread pans.

7 ▲ Punch down the risen dough.

8 Divide the dough in half and form into loaves. Place in the pans, seam-side down. Dust the tops with flour.

9 Cover with plastic bags and leave to rise in a warm place until doubled in volume, about 1 hour.

10 Preheat the oven to 375°F.

11 ▼ Bake until the bottoms sound hollow when tapped, 45–50 minutes. Cool on racks.

Whole-Wheat Buttermilk Rolls

MAKES 12

2 teaspoons active dry yeast
¼ cup lukewarm water
1 teaspoon sugar
¾ cup lukewarm buttermilk
¼ teaspoon baking soda
1 teaspoon salt
3 tablespoons butter, at room temperature
1½ cups whole-wheat flour
1 cup all-purpose flour
1 beaten egg, for glazing

1 In a large bowl, combine the yeast, water, and sugar. Stir, and leave for 15 minutes to dissolve.

2 ▲ Add the buttermilk, baking soda, salt, and butter and stir to blend. Stir in the whole-wheat flour.

3 Add just enough of the all-purpose flour to obtain a rough dough. If the dough is stiff, stir with your hands.

4 Transfer to a floured surface and knead until smooth and elastic. Divide into 3 equal parts. Roll each into a cylinder, then cut in 4.

5 ▼ Form the pieces into torpedo shapes. Place on a greased baking sheet, cover, and leave in a warm place until doubled in volume.

6 Preheat the oven to 400°F. Brush with the glaze. Bake until firm, 15–20 minutes. Cool on a rack.

French Bread

MAKES 2 LOAVES

1 package active dry yeast
2 cups lukewarm water
1 tablespoon salt
6–8 cups flour
cornmeal, for sprinkling

1 Combine the yeast and water, stir, and leave for 15 minutes to dissolve. Stir in the salt.

2 Add the flour, 1 cup at a time. Beat in with a wooden spoon, adding just enough flour to obtain a smooth dough. Alternatively, use an electric mixer with a dough hook attachment.

3 Transfer to a floured surface and knead until smooth and elastic.

4 Shape into a ball, place in a greased bowl, and cover with a plastic bag. Leave to rise in a warm place until doubled in volume, 2–4 hours.

5 ▲ Transfer to a lightly floured board and shape into two long loaves. Place on a baking sheet sprinkled with cornmeal, let rise for 5 minutes.

6 ▲ Score the tops in several places with a very sharp knife. Brush with water and place in a cold oven. Set a pan of boiling water on the bottom of the oven and set the oven to 400°F. Bake until crusty and golden, about 40 minutes. Cool on a rack.

Whole-Wheat Buttermilk Rolls (top), French Bread

Butter-Poppy Seed Knots

MAKES 12

1¼ cups lukewarm milk

4 tablespoons butter, at room temperature

1 teaspoon sugar

2 teaspoons active dry yeast

1 egg yolk

2 teaspoons salt

3½–4 cups flour

1 egg beaten with 2 teaspoons of water, for glazing

poppy seeds, for sprinkling

1 In a large bowl, stir together the milk, butter, sugar, and yeast. Leave for 15 minutes to dissolve.

2 Stir in the egg yolk, salt, and 2 cups flour. Add 1 cup of flour and stir to obtain a soft dough.

3 Transfer to a floured surface and knead, adding flour if necessary, until smooth and elastic. Place in a bowl, cover, and leave in a warm place until doubled in volume, 1½–2 hours.

4 ▲ Grease a baking sheet. Punch down the dough with your fist and cut into 12 pieces the size of golf balls.

5 ▲ Roll each piece to a rope, twist to form a knot and place 1 inch apart on the baking sheet. Cover loosely and leave to rise in a warm place until doubled in volume, 1–1½ hours.

6 Preheat the oven to 350°F.

7 ▲ Brush the knots with the egg glaze and sprinkle over the poppy seeds. Bake until the tops are lightly browned, 25–30 minutes. Cool slightly on a rack before serving.

Clover Leaf Rolls

MAKES 24

1¼ cups milk
2 tablespoons sugar
4 tablespoons butter, at room temperature,
2 teaspoons active dry yeast
1 egg
2 teaspoons salt
3½–4 cups flour
melted butter, for glazing

4 Grease 2 12-cup muffin pans.

5 ▼ Punch down the dough. Cut into 4 equal pieces. Roll each piece into a rope 14 inches long. Cut each rope into 18 pieces, then roll each into a ball.

6 ▲ Place 3 balls, side by side, in each muffin cup. Cover loosely and leave to rise in a warm place until doubled in volume, about 1½ hours.

7 Preheat the oven to 400°F.

8 Brush with glaze. Bake until lightly browned, about 20 minutes. Cool slightly before serving.

1 ▲ Heat the milk until lukewarm; test the temperature with your knuckle. Pour into a large bowl, and stir in the sugar, butter, and yeast. Leave for 15 minutes to dissolve.

2 Stir the egg and salt into the yeast mixture. Gradually stir in 3½ cups of the flour. Add just enough extra flour to obtain a rough dough.

3 ▲ Transfer to a floured surface and knead until smooth and elastic. Place in a greased bowl, cover, and leave in a warm place until doubled in volume, about 1½ hours.

Parker House Rolls

MAKES 48 ROLLS

1 package active dry yeast
2 cups lukewarm milk
½ cup margarine
5 tablespoons sugar
2 teaspoons salt
2 eggs
7–8 cups flour
4 tablespoons butter

1 Combine the yeast and ½ cup milk in a large bowl. Stir and leave for 15 minutes to dissolve.

2 Bring the remaining milk to a simmer, cool for 5 minutes, then beat in the margarine, sugar, salt, and eggs. Let cool to lukewarm.

3 ▲ Pour the milk mixture into the yeast mixture. Stir in 4 cups of flour with a wooden spoon. Add the remaining flour, 1 cup at a time, until a rough dough is obtained.

4 Transfer the dough to a lightly floured surface and knead until smooth and elastic. Place in a clean bowl, cover with a plastic bag, and leave to rise in a warm place until doubled in volume, about 2 hours.

5 In a saucepan, melt the butter and set aside. Grease 2 baking sheets.

6 Punch down the dough and divide into 4 equal pieces. Roll each piece into an 8- × 12-inch rectangle, about ¼ inch thick.

7 ▲ Cut each of the rectangles into 4 2- × 12-inch strips. Cut each strip into 3 4- × 2-inch rectangles.

8 ▲ Brush each rectangle with melted butter, then fold the rectangles in half, so that the top extends about ½ inch over the bottom.

9 ▲ Place the rolls slightly overlapping on the baking sheet, with the longer side facing up.

10 Cover and refrigerate for 30 minutes. Preheat the oven to 350°F. Bake until golden, 18–20 minutes. Cool the rolls slightly before serving.

Bread Sticks

MAKES 18–20

1 package active dry yeast
1¼ cups lukewarm water
3 cups flour
2 teaspoons salt
1 teaspoon sugar
2 tablespoons olive oil
1 cup sesame seeds
1 beaten egg, for glazing
coarse salt, for sprinkling

1 Combine the yeast and water, stir, and leave for 15 minutes to dissolve.

2 ▲ Place the flour, salt, sugar, and olive oil in a food processor. With the motor running, slowly pour in the yeast mixture and process until the dough forms a ball. If sticky, add more flour; if dry, add more water.

3 Transfer to a floured surface and knead until smooth and elastic. Place in a bowl, cover, and leave to rise in a warm place for 45 minutes.

4 ▲ Lightly toast the sesame seeds in a skillet. Grease 2 baking sheets.

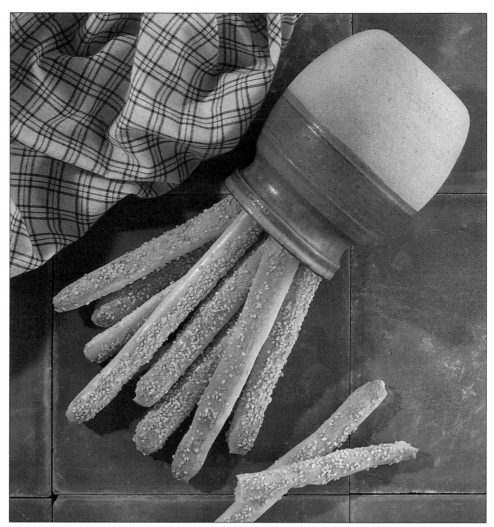

5 ▼ Roll small handfuls of dough into cylinders, about 12 inches long. Place on the baking sheets.

~ **VARIATION** ~

If preferred, use other seeds, such as poppy or caraway, or for plain bread sticks, omit the seeds and salt.

6 ▲ Brush with egg glaze, sprinkle with the sesame seeds, then sprinkle over some coarse salt. Leave to rise, uncovered, until almost doubled in volume, about 20 minutes.

7 Preheat the oven to 400°F. Bake until golden, about 15 minutes. Turn off the heat but leave the bread sticks in the oven for 5 minutes more. Serve warm or cool.

Sticky Buns

MAKES 18

⅔ cup milk

1 package active dry yeast

2 tablespoons granulated sugar

3–3¼ cups flour

1 teaspoon salt

½ cup (1 stick) cold butter, cut in pieces

2 eggs, lightly beaten

grated rind of 1 lemon

FOR THE TOPPING AND FILLING

1¼ cups dark brown sugar, firmly
  packed

5 tablespoons butter

½ cup water

¾ cup pecans, chopped

3 tablespoons granulated sugar

2 teaspoons ground cinnamon

¾ cup raisins

1 Heat the milk to lukewarm. Add the yeast and sugar and leave until frothy, about 15 minutes.

2 Combine the flour and salt in a large mixing bowl. Add the butter and cut in with a pastry blender until the mixture resembles coarse crumbs.

3 ▲ Make a well in the center and add the yeast mixture, eggs, and lemon rind. With a wooden spoon, stir from the center, incorporating flour with each turn. When it becomes too stiff, stir by hand to obtain a rough dough.

4 Transfer to a floured surface and knead until smooth and elastic. Return to the bowl, cover with a plastic bag, and leave to rise in a warm place until doubled in volume, about 2 hours.

5 Meanwhile, for the topping, make the syrup. Combine the brown sugar, butter, and water in a heavy saucepan. Bring to a boil and boil gently until thick and syrupy, about 10 minutes.

6 ▲ Place 1 tablespoon of the syrup in the bottom of each of 18 1½-inch muffin cups. Sprinkle in a thin layer of chopped pecans, reserving the rest for the filling.

7 Punch down the dough and transfer to a floured surface. Roll out to an 18- × 12-inch rectangle.

8 ▲ For the filling, combine the granulated sugar, cinnamon, raisins, and reserved nuts. Sprinkle over the dough in an even layer.

9 ▲ Roll up tightly, from the long side, to form a cylinder.

10 ▲ Cut the cylinder into 1-inch rounds. Place each in a prepared muffin cup, cut-side up. Leave to rise in a warm place until increased by half, about 30 minutes.

11 Preheat the oven to 350°F. Place a sheet of foil under the pans to catch any syrup that bubbles over. Bake until golden, about 25 minutes.

12 Remove from the oven and invert the pans onto a sheet of wax paper. Leave for 3–5 minutes, then remove buns from the pans. Transfer to a rack to cool. Serve sticky-side up.

~ COOK'S TIP ~

To save time and energy, make double the recipe and freeze half for another occasion.

Prune-Filled Coffee Cake

MAKES 1 LOAF

1 package active dry yeast
¼ cup lukewarm water
¼ cup lukewarm milk
¼ cup sugar
½ teaspoon salt
1 egg
4 tablespoons butter, at room temperature
3–3½ cups flour
1 egg beaten with 2 teaspoons water, for glazing

FOR THE FILLING

1 cup cooked prunes
2 teaspoons grated lemon rind
1 teaspoon grated orange rind
¼ teaspoon freshly grated nutmeg
3 tablespoons butter, melted
½ cup walnuts, very finely chopped
2 tablespoons sugar

1 In a large bowl, combine the yeast and water, stir, and leave for 15 minutes to dissolve.

2 Stir in the milk, sugar, salt, egg, and butter. Gradually stir in 2½ cups of the flour to obtain a soft dough.

3 Transfer to a floured surface and knead in just enough flour to obtain a dough that is smooth and elastic. Put into a clean bowl, cover, and leave to rise in a warm place until doubled in volume, about 1½ hours.

~ VARIATION ~

For Apricot-Filled Coffee Cake, replace the prunes with the same amount of dried apricots. It is not necessary to cook them, but to soften, soak them in hot tea and discard the liquid before using.

---

4 ▲ Meanwhile, for the filling, combine the prunes, lemon and orange rinds, nutmeg, butter, walnuts, and sugar and stir to blend. Set aside.

5 Grease a large baking sheet. Punch down the dough and transfer to a lightly floured surface. Knead briefly, then roll out into a 15- × 10-inch rectangle. Carefully transfer to the baking sheet.

6 ▲ Spread the filling in the center.

7 ▲ With a sharp knife, cut 10 strips at an angle on either side of the filling, cutting just to the filling.

8 ▲ For a braided pattern, fold up one end neatly, then fold over the strips from alternating sides until all the strips are folded over. Tuck excess dough at ends underneath.

9 ▲ Cover loosely with a dish towel and leave to rise in a warm place until almost doubled in volume.

10 ▲ Preheat the oven to 375°F. Brush with the glaze. Bake until browned, about 30 minutes. Transfer to a rack to cool.

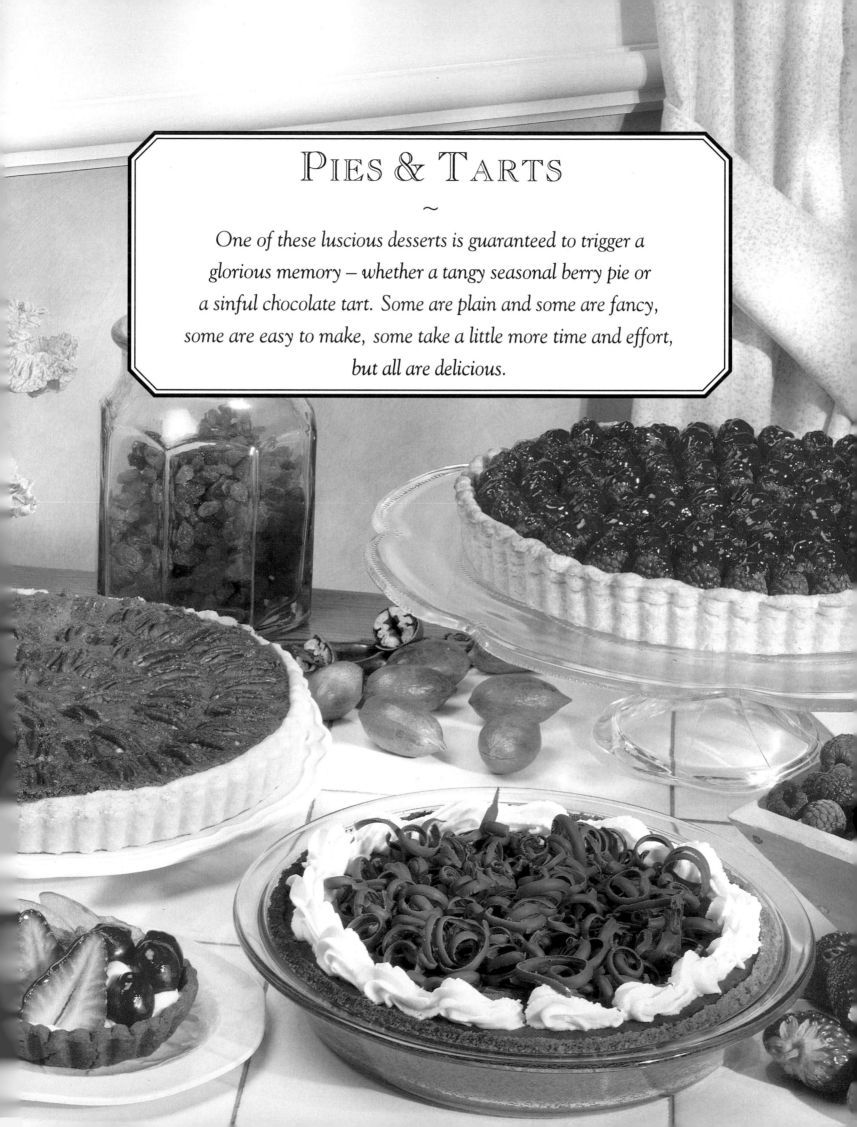

PIES & TARTS

~

*One of these luscious desserts is guaranteed to trigger a
glorious memory – whether a tangy seasonal berry pie or
a sinful chocolate tart. Some are plain and some are fancy,
some are easy to make, some take a little more time and effort,
but all are delicious.*

Apple Pie

SERVES 8

2 pounds tart cooking apples

2 tablespoons flour

½ cup sugar

1½ tablespoons fresh lemon juice

½ teaspoon ground cinnamon

½ teaspoon ground allspice

¼ teaspoon ground ginger

¼ teaspoon grated nutmeg

¼ teaspoon salt

4 tablespoons butter, diccd

FOR THE CRUST

2 cups flour

1 teaspoon salt

6 tablespoons cold butter, cut in pieces

4 tablespoons cold shortening, cut in pieces

¼–½ cup ice water

1 ▲ For the crust, sift the flour and salt into a bowl.

2 Add the butter and shortening and cut in with a pastry blender or rub between your fingertips until the mixture resembles coarse crumbs. With a fork, stir in just enough water to bind the dough.

3 ▲ Gather into 2 balls, wrap in wax paper and refrigerate for 20 minutes.

4 ▲ On a lightly floured surface, roll out 1 dough ball ⅛ inch thick. Transfer to a 9-inch pie pan and trim the edge. Place a baking sheet in the center of the oven and preheat to 425°F.

5 ▲ Peel, core, and slice the apples into a bowl. Toss with the flour, sugar, lemon juice, spices, and salt. Spoon into pie shell; dot with butter.

6 ▲ Roll out the remaining dough. Place on top of the pie and trim to leave a ¾-inch overhang. Fold the overhang under the bottom dough and press to seal. Crimp the edge.

7 ▲ Roll out the scraps and cut out leaf shapes and roll balls. Arrange on top of the pie. Cut steam vents.

8 Bake for 10 minutes. Reduce the heat to 350°F and bake until golden, 40–45 minutes more. If the pie browns too quickly, protect with foil.

~ **COOK'S TIP** ~

Select apples that are firm and tart, such as Jonathan, Greening, Granny Smith or Winesap. Macintosh and Delicious soften too much during cooking.

Apple-Cranberry Lattice Pie

SERVES 8

grated rind of 1 orange

3 tablespoons fresh orange juice

2 large, tart cooking apples

1 cup cranberries

½ cup raisins

¼ cup walnuts, chopped

1 cup plus tablespoon granulated sugar

½ cup dark brown sugar, firmly packed

1 tablespoon quick-cooking tapioca

FOR THE CRUST

2 cups flour

½ teaspoon salt

6 tablespoons cold butter, cut in pieces

4 tablespoons cold shortening, cut in pieces

¼–½ cup ice water

1 ▼ For the crust, sift the flour and salt into a bowl. Add the butter and shortening and rub with your fingertips until the mixture resembles coarse crumbs, or use a pastry blender. With a fork, stir in just enough water to bind the dough. Gather into 2 equal balls, wrap in wax paper, and refrigerate for at least 20 minutes.

2 ▲ Put the orange rind and juice into a mixing bowl. Peel and core the apples and grate them into the bowl. Stir in the cranberries, raisins, walnuts, 1 cup of the granulated sugar, brown sugar, and tapioca.

3 Place a baking sheet in the oven and preheat to 400°F.

4 On a lightly floured surface, roll out 1 ball of dough about ⅛ inch thick. Transfer to a 9-inch pie pan and trim the edge. Spoon the cranberry and apple mixture into the shell.

5 ▲ Roll out the remaining dough to a circle about 11 inches in diameter. With a serrated pastry wheel, cut the dough into 10 strips, ¾ inch wide. Place 5 strips horizontally across the top of the tart at 1-inch intervals. Weave in 5 vertical strips. Trim the edges. Sprinkle the top with the remaining 1 tablespoon sugar.

6 Bake for 20 minutes. Reduce the heat to 350°F and bake until the crust is golden and the filling is bubbling, about 15 minutes more.

Blueberry Pie

SERVES 8

1 pound blueberries
½ cup sugar
3 tablespoons cornstarch
2 tablespoons fresh lemon juice
2 tablespoons butter, diced
FOR THE CRUST
2 cups flour
¾ teaspoon salt
½ cup (1 stick) cold butter, cut in pieces
3 tablespoons cold shortening, cut in pieces
5–6 tablespoons ice water
1 egg beaten with 1 tablespoon water, for glazing

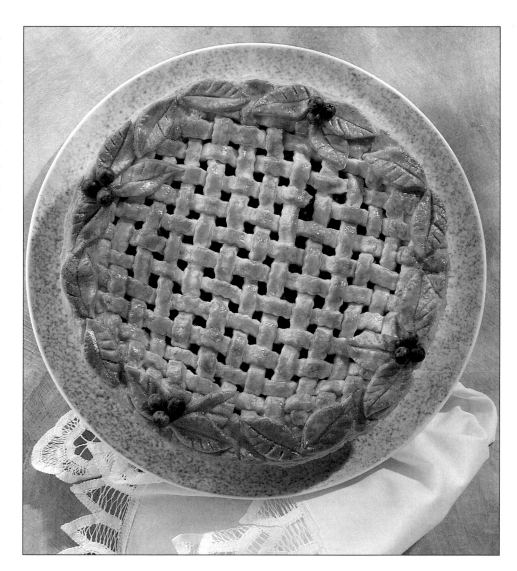

1 For the crust, sift the flour and salt into a bowl. Add the butter and shortening and cut in with a pastry blender until the mixture resembles coarse crumbs. With a fork, stir in just enough water to bind the dough. Gather into 2 equal balls, wrap in wax paper, and refrigerate for 20 minutes.

2 On a lightly floured surface, roll out one dough ball about ⅛ inch thick. Transfer to a 9-inch pie pan and trim to leave a ½-inch overhang. Brush the bottom with egg glaze.

3 ▲ Mix all the filling ingredients together, except the butter (reserve a few blueberries for decoration). Spoon into the shell and dot with the butter. Brush the egg glaze on the edge of the lower crust.

4 Place a baking sheet in the center of the oven and preheat to 425°F.

5 ▼ Roll out the remaining dough on a baking tray lined with wax paper. With a serrated pastry wheel, cut out 24 thin strips of dough. Roll out the scraps and cut out leaf shapes. Mark veins in the leaves with the point of a knife.

6 ▲ Weave the strips in a close lattice, then transfer to the pie using the wax paper. Press the edges to seal and trim. Arrange the dough leaves around the rim. Brush with egg glaze.

7 Bake for 10 minutes. Reduce the heat to 350°F and bake until the pastry is golden, 40–45 minutes more. Decorate with reserved blueberries.

Pear-Apple Crumb Pie

SERVES 8

3 firm pears

4 tart cooking apples

¾ cup sugar

2 tablespoons cornstarch

⅛ teaspoon salt

grated rind of 1 lemon

2 tablespoons fresh lemon juice

½ cup raisins

¾ cup flour

1 teaspoon ground cinnamon

6 tablespoons cold butter, cut in pieces

FOR THE CRUST

1 cup flour

½ teaspoon salt

⅓ cup cold shortening, cut in pieces

2 tablespoons ice water

1 For the crust, combine the flour and salt in a bowl. Add the shortening and cut in with a pastry blender until the mixture resembles coarse crumbs. With a fork, stir in just enough water to bind the dough. Gather into a ball and transfer to a lightly floured surface. Roll out about ⅛ inch thick.

2 ▲ Transfer to a shallow 9-inch pie pan and trim to leave a ½-inch overhang. Fold the overhang under for a double thickness. Flute the edge with your fingers. Refrigerate.

3 Place a baking sheet in the oven and preheat to 450°F.

4 ▲ Peel and core the pears. Slice them into a bowl. Peel, core, and slice the apples. Add to the pears. Stir in ⅓ cup of the sugar, the cornstarch, salt, and lemon rind. Add the lemon juice and raisins and stir to blend.

5 For the crumb topping, combine the remaining sugar, flour, cinnamon, and butter in a bowl. Blend with your fingertips until the mixture resembles coarse crumbs. Set aside.

6 ▲ Spoon the fruit filling into the pie shell. Sprinkle the crumbs lightly and evenly over the top.

7 Bake for 10 minutes, then reduce the heat to 350°F. Cover the top of the pie loosely with a sheet of foil and continue baking until browned, 35–40 minutes more.

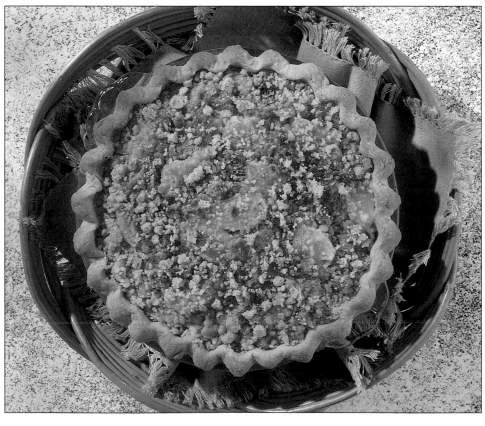

Rhubarb Cherry Pie

SERVES 8

1 pound rhubarb, cut into 1-inch pieces (about 3 cups)

1 1-pound can (2 cups) pitted tart red or black cherries, drained

1¼ cups sugar

¼ cup quick-cooking tapioca

FOR THE CRUST

2 cups flour

1 teaspoon salt

6 tablespoons cold butter, cut in pieces

4 tablespoons cold shortening, cut in pieces

¼–½ cup ice water

milk, for glazing

1 ▲ For the crust, sift the flour and salt into a bowl. Add the butter and shortening to the dry ingredients and cut in with a pastry blender until the mixture resembles coarse crumbs.

2 With a fork, stir in just enough water to bind the dough. Gather the dough into 2 balls, one slightly larger than the other. Wrap the dough in wax paper and refrigerate for at least 20 minutes.

3 Place a baking sheet in the center of the oven and preheat to 400°F.

4 On a lightly floured surface, roll out the larger dough ball to a thickness of about ⅛ inch.

5 ▼ Roll the dough around the rolling pin and transfer to a 9-inch pie pan. Trim the edge to leave a ½-inch overhang all around.

6 Refrigerate the pie shell while making the filling.

7 In a mixing bowl, combine the rhubarb, cherries, sugar, and tapioca and spoon into the pie shell.

8 ▲ Roll out the remaining dough and cut out leaf shapes.

9 Transfer the dough to the pie and trim to leave a ¾-inch overhang. Fold the top edge under the bottom and flute. Roll small balls from the scraps. Mark veins in the dough leaves and place on top with the dough balls.

10 Glaze the top and bake until golden, 40–50 minutes.

Peach Leaf Pie

SERVES 8

2½ pounds ripe peaches

juice of 1 lemon

½ cup sugar

3 tablespoons cornstarch

¼ teaspoon grated nutmeg

½ teaspoon ground cinnamon

2 tablespoons butter, diced

FOR THE CRUST

2 cups flour

¾ teaspoon salt

½ cup (1 stick) cold butter, cut in pieces

3 tablespoons cold shortening, cut in pieces

5–6 tablespoons ice water

1 egg beaten with 1 tablespoon water, for glazing

1 For the crust, sift the flour and salt into a bowl. Add the butter and shortening and cut in with a pastry blender until the mixture resembles coarse crumbs.

2 ▲ With a fork, stir in just enough water to bind the dough. Gather into 2 balls, one slightly larger than the other. Wrap in wax paper and refrigerate for at least 20 minutes.

3 Place a baking sheet in the oven and preheat to 425°F.

4 ▲ Drop a few peaches at a time into boiling water for 20 seconds, then transfer to a bowl of cold water. When cool, peel off the skins.

5 Slice the peaches and combine with the lemon juice, sugar, cornstarch, and spices. Set aside.

6 ▲ On a lightly floured surface, roll out the larger dough ball about ⅛ inch thick. Transfer to a 9-inch pie pan and trim the edge. Refrigerate.

7 ▲ Roll out the remaining dough ¼ inch thick. Cut out leaf shapes 3 inches long, using a template if needed. Mark veins with a knife. With the scraps, roll a few balls.

8 ▲ Brush the bottom of the pie shell with egg glaze. Add the peaches, piling them higher in the center. Dot with the butter.

9 ▲ To assemble, start from the outside edge and cover the peaches with a ring of leaves. Place a second ring of leaves above, staggering the positions. Continue with rows of leaves until covered. Place the balls in the center. Brush with glaze.

10 Bake for 10 minutes. Lower the heat to 350°F and continue to bake for 35–40 minutes more.

~ COOK'S TIP ~

Baking the pie on a preheated baking sheet helps to make the bottom crust crisp. The moisture from the filling keeps the bottom crust more humid than the top, but this baking method helps to compensate for the top crust being better exposed to the heat source.

Raspberry Tart

SERVES 8

4 egg yolks

⅓ cup sugar

3 tablespoons flour

1¼ cups milk

⅛ teaspoon salt

½ teaspoon vanilla extract

1 pound fresh raspberries (about 1 quart)

5 tablespoons concord grape jelly

1 tablespoon fresh orange juice

FOR THE CRUST

1¼ cups flour

½ teaspoon baking powder

¼ teaspoon salt

1 tablespoon sugar

grated rind of ½ orange

6 tablespoons cold butter, cut in pieces

1 egg yolk

3–4 tablespoons whipping cream

1 For the crust, sift the flour, baking powder, and salt into a bowl. Stir in the sugar and orange rind. Add the butter and cut in with a pastry blender until the mixture resembles coarse crumbs. With a fork, stir in the egg yolk and just enough cream to bind the dough. Gather into a ball, wrap in wax paper, and refrigerate.

2 For the custard filling, beat the egg yolks and sugar until thick and lemon-colored. Gradually stir in the flour.

3 In a saucepan, bring the milk and salt just to the boil, and remove from the heat. Whisk into the egg yolk mixture, return to the pan, and continue whisking over moderately high heat until just bubbling. Cook for 3 minutes to thicken. Transfer immediately to a bowl. Add the vanilla and stir to blend.

4 ▲ Cover with wax paper to prevent a skin from forming.

5 ▲ Preheat the oven to 400°F. On a lightly floured surface, roll out the dough about ⅛ inch thick, transfer to a 10-inch tart pan and trim the edge. Prick the bottom all over with a fork and line with crumpled wax paper. Fill with pie weights and bake for 15 minutes. Remove the paper and weights. Continue baking until golden, 6–8 minutes more. Let cool.

6 ▲ Spread an even layer of the pastry cream filling in the tart shell and arrange the raspberries on top. Melt the jelly and orange juice in a pan and brush on top to glaze.

Cherry Strudel

SERVES 8

2 cups fresh bread crumbs
¾ cup (1½ sticks) butter, melted
1 cup sugar
1 tablespoon ground cinnamon
1 teaspoon grated lemon rind
4 cups sour cherries, pitted
8 sheets phyllo pastry
confectioners' sugar, for dusting

1 Lightly fry the bread crumbs in 5 tablespoons of the butter until golden. Set aside to cool.

2 ▲ In a large mixing bowl, toss together the sugar, cinnamon, and lemon rind.

3 Stir in the cherries.

4 Preheat the oven to 375°F. Grease a baking sheet.

5 Carefully unfold the phyllo sheets. Keep the unused sheets covered with wax paper. Lift off one sheet, place on a flat surface lined with wax paper. Brush the pastry with melted butter. Sprinkle bread crumbs evenly over the surface, using about ¼ cup of crumbs.

6 ▲ Lay a second sheet of phyllo on top, brush with butter and sprinkle with crumbs. Continue until you have a stack of 8 buttered sheets.

7 Spoon the cherry mixture at the bottom edge of the strip. Starting at the cherry-filled end, roll up the dough as for a jelly roll. Use the wax paper to help flip the strudel on to the baking sheet, seam-side down.

8 ▼ Carefully fold under the ends to seal in the fruit. Brush the top with any remaining butter.

9 Bake the strudel for 45 minutes. Let cool slightly. Using a small sieve, dust with a fine layer of confectioners' sugar. Serve warm.

Key Lime Pie

SERVES 8

3 large egg yolks

1 14-ounce can sweetened condensed milk

1 tablespoon grated Key lime rind

½ cup fresh Key lime juice

green food coloring (optional)

½ cup whipping cream

FOR THE CRUST

1¼ cups graham cracker crumbs

5 tablespoons butter or margarine, melted

1 Preheat the oven to 350°F.

2 ▲ For the crust, place the graham cracker crumbs in a bowl and add the butter or margarine. Mix to combine.

~ **VARIATION** ~

If Key limes are not available, use regular limes.

3 Press the crumbs evenly over the bottom and sides of a 9-inch pie pan. Bake for 8 minutes. Let cool.

4 ▲ Beat the yolks until thick. Beat in the milk, lime rind and juice, and coloring, if using. Pour into the prebaked pie shell and refrigerate until set, about 4 hours. To serve, whip the cream. Pipe a lattice pattern on top, or spoon dollops around the edge.

Fruit Tartlets

MAKES 8

¾ cup red currant or grape jelly

1 tablespoon fresh lemon juice

¾ cup whipping cream

1½ pounds fresh fruit, such as strawberries, raspberries, kiwi fruit, peaches, grapes, or blueberries, peeled and sliced as necessary

FOR THE CRUST

⅔ cup (10⅔ tablespoons) cold butter, cut in pieces

⅓ cup dark brown sugar, firmly packed

3 tablespoons unsweetened cocoa powder

1½ cups flour

1 egg white

1 For the crust, combine the butter, brown sugar, and cocoa over low heat. When the butter is melted, remove from the heat and sift over the flour. Stir, then add just enough egg white to bind the mixture. Gather into a ball, wrap in wax paper, and refrigerate for at least 30 minutes.

2 ▲ Grease 8 3-inch tartlet pans. Roll out the dough between two sheets of wax paper. Stamp out 8 4-inch rounds with a fluted cutter.

3 Line the tartlet pans with dough. Prick the bottoms. Refrigerate for 15 minutes. Preheat the oven to 350°F.

4 Bake until firm, 20–25 minutes. Cool, then remove from the pans.

5 ▲ Melt the jelly with the lemon juice. Brush a thin layer in the bottom of the tartlets. Whip the cream and spread a thin layer in the tartlet shells. Arrange the fruit on top. Brush with the glaze and serve.

Key Lime Pie (top), Fruit Tartlets

Lemon Meringue Pie

SERVES 8

grated rind and juice of 1 large lemon
1 cup plus 1 tablespoon cold water
½ cup plus 6 tablespoons sugar
2 tablespoons butter
3 tablespoons cornstarch
3 eggs, separated
⅛ teaspoon salt
⅛ teaspoon cream of tartar
FOR THE CRUST
1 cup flour
½ teaspoon salt
⅓ cup (5⅓ tablespoons) cold shortening, cut in pieces
2 tablespoons ice water

1 For the crust, sift the flour and salt into a bowl. Add the shortening and cut in with a pastry blender until the mixture resembles coarse crumbs. With a fork, stir in just enough water to bind the dough. Gather the dough into a ball.

2 ▲ On a lightly floured surface, roll out the dough about ⅛ inch thick. Transfer to a 9-inch pie pan and trim the edge to leave a ½-inch overhang.

3 ▲ Fold the overhang under and crimp the edge. Refrigerate the pie shell for at least 20 minutes.

4 Preheat the oven to 400°F.

5 ▲ Prick the dough all over with a fork. Line with crumpled wax paper and fill with pie weights. Bake for 12 minutes. Remove the paper and weights and continue baking until golden, 6–8 minutes more.

6 In a saucepan, combine the lemon rind and juice, 1 cup of the water, ½ cup of the sugar, and butter. Bring the mixture to a boil.

7 Meanwhile, in a mixing bowl, dissolve the cornstarch in the remaining water. Add the egg yolks.

~ VARIATION ~

For Lime Meringue Pie, substitute the grated rind and juice of 2 medium-sized limes for the lemon.

---

8 ▲ Add the egg yolks to the lemon mixture and return to a boil, whisking continuously until the mixture thickens, about 5 minutes.

9 Cover the surface with wax paper to prevent a skin forming and let cool.

10 ▲ For the meringue, using an electric mixer beat the egg whites with the salt and cream of tartar until they hold stiff peaks. Add the remaining sugar and beat until glossy.

11 ▲ Spoon the lemon mixture into the pie shell and spread level. Spoon the meringue on top, smoothing it up to the edge of the crust to seal. Bake until golden, 12–15 minutes.

Orange Tart

SERVES 8

1 cup sugar

1 cup fresh orange juice, strained

2 large navel oranges

¾ cup blanched almonds

4 tablespoons butter

1 egg

1 tablespoon flour

3 tablespoons apricot jam

FOR THE CRUST

1½ cups flour

½ teaspoon salt

4 tablespoons cold butter, cut in pieces

3 tablespoons cold margarine, cut in pieces

3–4 tablespoons ice water

1 For the crust, sift the flour and salt into a bowl. Add the butter and margarine and cut in with a pastry blender until the mixture resembles coarse crumbs. Stir in just enough water to bind the dough. Gather into a ball, wrap in wax paper, and refrigerate for at least 20 minutes.

2 On a lightly floured surface, roll out the dough ¼ inch thick and transfer to an 8-inch tart pan. Trim off the overhang. Refrigerate until needed.

3 In a saucepan, combine ¾ cup of the sugar and the orange juice and boil until thick and syrupy, about 10 minutes.

4 ▲ Cut the oranges into ¼-inch slices. Do not peel. Add to the syrup. Simmer gently for 10 minutes, or until glazed. Transfer to a rack to dry. When cool, cut in half. Reserve the syrup. Place a baking sheet in the oven and heat to 400°F.

5 Grind the almonds finely in a food processor, blender or nut grinder. With an electric mixer, cream the butter and remaining sugar until light and fluffy. Beat in the egg and 2 tablespoons of the orange syrup. Stir in the almonds and flour.

6 Melt the jam over low heat, then brush in the tart shell. Pour in the almond mixture. Bake until set, about 20 minutes. Let cool.

7 ▲ Arrange overlapping orange slices on top. Boil the remaining syrup until thick. Brush on top to glaze.

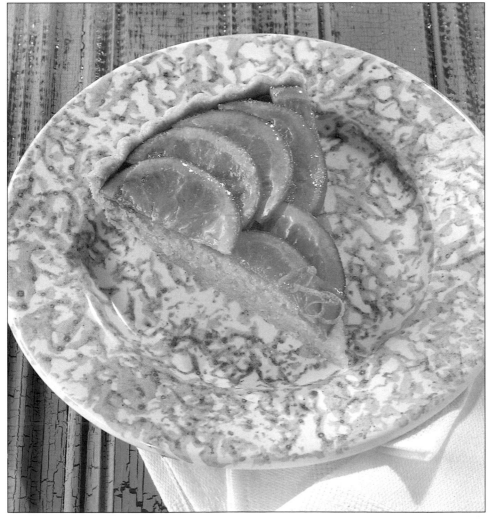

Pecan Tart

SERVES 8

3 eggs

⅛ teaspoon of salt

1 cup dark brown sugar, firmly packed

½ cup dark corn syrup

2 tablespoons fresh lemon juice

6 tablespoons butter, melted

1½ cups pecans, chopped

½ cup pecan halves

FOR THE CRUST

1¼ cups flour

1 tablespoon granulated sugar

1 teaspoon baking powder

½ teaspoon salt

6 tablespoons cold unsalted butter, cut in pieces

1 egg yolk

3–4 tablespoons whipping cream

1 For the crust, sift the flour, sugar, baking powder, and salt into a bowl. Add the butter and cut in with a pastry blender until the mixture resembles coarse crumbs.

2 ▼ In a bowl, beat together the egg yolk and cream until blended.

~ **COOK'S TIP** ~

Serve this tart warm, accompanied by ice cream or whipped cream, if wished.

3 ▲ Pour the cream mixture into the flour mixture and stir with a fork.

4 Gather the dough into a ball. On a lightly floured surface, roll out ⅛ inch thick and transfer to a 9-inch tart pan. Trim the overhang and flute the edge with your fingers. Refrigerate for at least 20 minutes.

5 Set a baking sheet in the middle of the oven and preheat to 400°F.

6 In a bowl, lightly whisk the eggs and salt. Add the sugar, corn syrup, lemon juice, and butter. Mix well and stir in the chopped nuts.

7 ▲ Pour into the pastry shell and arrange the pecan halves in concentric circles on top.

8 Bake for 10 minutes. Reduce the heat to 325°F; continue baking 25 minutes more.

Chess Pie

SERVES 8

2 eggs
3 tablespoons whipping cream
½ cup dark brown sugar, firmly packed
2 tablespoons granulated sugar
2 tablespoons flour
1 tablespoon bourbon or whisky
3 tablespoons butter, melted
½ cup walnuts, chopped
¾ cup pitted dates
whipped cream, for serving

FOR THE CRUST

6 tablespoons cold butter
3 tablespoons cold shortening
1½ cups flour
½ teaspoon salt
3–4 tablespoons ice water

1 ▲ For the crust, cut the butter and shortening in small pieces.

2 Sift the flour and salt into a bowl. With a pastry blender, cut in the butter and margarine until the mixture resembles coarse crumbs. Stir in just enough water to bind. Gather into a ball, wrap in wax paper, and refrigerate for at least 20 minutes.

3 Place a baking sheet in the center of the oven and preheat to 375°F.

4 Roll out the dough ⅛ inch thick. Transfer to a 9-inch pie pan and trim the edge. Roll out the trimmings, cut thin strips and braid them. Brush the edge of the pie with water and place the dough braid around the edge.

5 ▲ In a mixing bowl, whisk together the eggs and cream.

6 Add both sugars and beat until well combined. Sift over 1 tablespoon of the flour and stir in. Add the bourbon or whisky, the melted butter, and the walnuts. Stir to combine.

7 ▲ Mix the dates with the remaining tablespoon of flour and stir into the walnut mixture.

8 Pour into the pie shell and bake until the pastry is golden and the filling puffed up, about 35 minutes. Serve at room temperature, with whipped cream if desired.

Coconut Cream Pie

SERVES 8

2½ cups flaked sweetened coconut

⅔ cup sugar

4 tablespoons cornstarch

⅛ teaspoon salt

2½ cups milk

¼ cup whipping cream

2 egg yolks

2 tablespoons unsalted butter

2 teaspoons vanilla extract

FOR THE CRUST

1 cup flour

¼ teaspoon salt

3 tablespoons cold butter, cut in pieces

2 tablespoons cold shortening

2–3 tablespoons ice water

1 For the crust, sift the flour and salt into a bowl. Add the butter and shortening and cut in with a pastry blender until the mixture resembles coarse crumbs.

2 ▲ With a fork, stir in just enough water to bind the dough. Gather into a ball, wrap in wax paper, and refrigerate for at least 20 minutes.

3 Preheat the oven to 425°F. Roll out the dough ⅛ inch thick. Transfer to a 9-inch pie pan. Trim and flute the edges. Prick the bottom. Line with crumpled wax paper and fill with pie weights. Bake for 10–12 minutes. Remove the paper and weights, reduce the heat to 350°F and bake until brown, 10–15 minutes more.

4 ▲ Spread 1 cup of the coconut on a baking sheet and toast in the oven until golden, 6–8 minutes, stirring often. Set aside for decorating.

5 Put the sugar, cornstarch, and salt in a saucepan. In a bowl, whisk the milk, cream, and egg yolks. Add the egg mixture to the saucepan.

6 ▼ Cook over low heat, stirring constantly, until the mixture comes to a boil. Boil for 1 minute, then remove from the heat. Add the butter, vanilla, and remaining coconut.

7 Pour into the prebaked pie shell. When cool, sprinkle toasted coconut in a ring in the center.

Black Bottom Pie

SERVES 8

2 teaspoons unflavored gelatin
3 tablespoons cold water
2 eggs, separated
1 cup sugar
2 tablespoons cornstarch
½ teaspoon salt
2 cups milk
2 1-ounce squares unsweetened chocolate, finely chopped
3 tablespoons rum
¼ teaspoon cream of tartar
chocolate curls, for decorating
FOR THE CRUST
1½ cups gingersnap cookie crumbs
⅓ cup (5⅓ tablespoons) butter, melted

1 Preheat the oven to 350°F.

2 For the crust, mix the cookie crumbs and melted butter.

3 ▲ Press the mixture evenly over the bottom and sides of a 9-inch pie pan. Bake for 6 minutes. Let cool.

4 Sprinkle the gelatin over the water and let stand to soften.

5 Beat the egg yolks in a large mixing bowl and set aside.

6 In a saucepan, combine half the sugar, the cornstarch, and salt. Gradually stir in the milk. Boil for 1 minute, stirring constantly.

7 ▲ Whisk the hot milk mixture into the yolks, then pour all back into the saucepan and return to a boil, whisking. Cook for 1 minute, still whisking. Remove from the heat.

8 ▲ Measure out 1 cup of the hot custard mixture and pour into a bowl. Add the chopped chocolate to the custard mixture, and stir until melted. Stir in half the rum and pour into the pie crust.

9 ▲ Whisk the softened gelatin into the plain custard until it has dissolved, then stir in the remaining rum. Set the pan in cold water until it reaches room temperature.

10 ▲ With an electric mixer, beat the egg whites and cream of tartar until they hold stiff peaks. Beat in half the remaining sugar until glossy, then fold in the rest of the sugar.

11 ▲ Fold the custard into the egg whites, then spoon over the chocolate mixture in the pie shell. Refrigerate until set, about 2 hours.

12 Decorate the top with chocolate curls. Keep the pie refrigerated until ready to serve.

~ COOK'S TIP ~

To make chocolate curls, melt 8 ounces semisweet chocolate over hot water, stir in 1 tablespoon of neutral vegetable oil, and mold in a small foil-lined loaf pan. For large curls, soften the bar between your hands and carve off curls from the wide side with a vegetable peeler; for small curls, grate from the narrow side using a box grater.

Shoofly Pie

SERVES 8

1 cup flour
½ cup dark brown sugar, firmly packed
¼ teaspoon each salt, ground ginger, cinnamon, mace, and grated nutmeg
6 tablespoons cold butter, cut in pieces
2 eggs
½ cup molasses
½ cup boiling water
½ teaspoon baking soda

FOR THE CRUST

4 ounces cream cheese, at room temperature, cut in pieces
½ cup (1 stick) cold butter, at room temperature, cut in pieces
1 cup flour

1 For the crust, put the cream cheese and butter in a mixing bowl. Sift over the flour.

2 ▲ Cut in with a pastry blender until the dough just holds together. Wrap in wax paper and refrigerate for at least 30 minutes.

3 Set a baking sheet in the center of the oven and preheat to 375°F.

4 In a bowl, mix together the flour, sugar, salt, spices, and cold butter pieces. Blend with your fingertips until the mixture resembles coarse crumbs. Set aside.

5 On a lightly floured surface, roll out the dough ⅛ inch thick and transfer to a 9-inch pie pan. Trim the overhang and flute the edges.

6 ▲ Spoon one-third of the crumbs into the pie shell.

7 ▲ To complete the filling, whisk the eggs with the molasses in a large bowl.

8 Measure the boiling water into a small bowl and stir in the soda; it will foam. Pour immediately into the egg mixture and whisk to blend. Pour carefully into the pie shell and sprinkle the remaining crumbs over the top in an even layer.

9 Bake on the hot sheet until browned, about 35 minutes. Let cool, then serve at room temperature.

Chocolate Chiffon Pie

SERVES 8

6 1-ounce squares semisweet chocolate

1 1-ounce square unsweetened chocolate

1 cup milk

1 tablespoon unflavored gelatin

⅔ cup sugar

2 extra-large eggs, separated

1 teaspoon vanilla extract

1½ cup whipping cream

⅛ teaspoon salt

whipped cream and chocolate curls, for decorating

FOR THE CRUST

1½ cups graham cracker crumbs

6 tablespoons butter, melted

6 ▲ Set the top of the double boiler in a bowl of ice and stir until the mixture reaches room temperature. Remove from the ice and set aside.

7 Whip the cream lightly. Set aside. With an electric mixer, beat the egg whites and salt until they hold soft peaks. Add the remaining sugar and beat only enough to blend.

8 Fold a dollop of egg whites into the chocolate mixture, then pour back into the whites and fold in.

9 ▲ Fold in the whipped cream and pour into the pastry shell. Put in the freezer until just set, about 5 minutes. If the center sinks, fill with any remaining mixture. Refrigerate for 3–4 hours. Decorate with whipped cream and chocolate curls. Serve cold.

1 Place a baking sheet in the oven and preheat to 350°F.

2 For the crust, mix the graham cracker crumbs and butter in a bowl. Press the crumbs evenly over the bottom and sides of a 9-inch pie pan. Bake for 8 minutes. Let cool.

3 Chop the chocolate, then grind in a food processor or blender. Set aside.

4 Place the milk in the top of a double boiler. Sprinkle over the gelatin. Let stand 5 minutes to soften.

5 ▲ Set the top of the double boiler over hot water. Add ⅓ cup of the sugar, the chocolate, and egg yolks. Stir until dissolved. Add the vanilla.

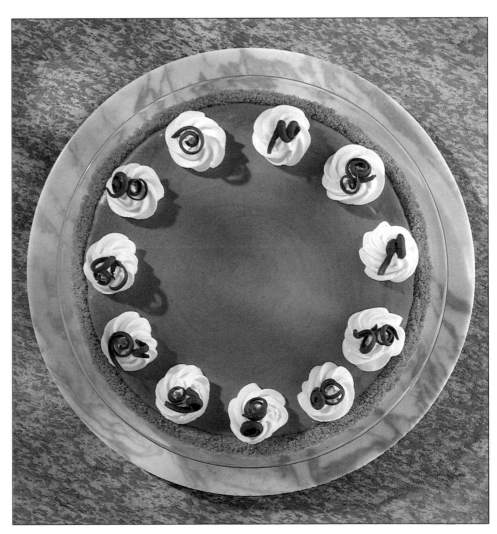

Chocolate Cheesecake Pie

SERVES 8

12 ounces cream cheese

4 tablespoons whipping cream

1 cup sugar

½ cup unsweetened cocoa powder

½ teaspoon ground cinnamon

3 eggs

whipped cream, for decorating

chocolate curls, for decorating

FOR THE CRUST

1 cup graham cracker crumbs

½ cup crushed amaretti cookies (if unavailable, use all graham cracker crumbs for a total of 1½ cups)

6 tablespoons butter, melted

1 Place a baking sheet in the oven and preheat to 350°F.

2 For the crust, mix the crumbs and butter in a bowl.

3 ▲ With a spoon, press the crumbs evenly over the bottom and sides of a 9-inch pie pan. Bake for 8 minutes. Let cool. Keep the oven on.

4 With an electric mixer, beat the cheese and cream together until smooth. Beat in the sugar, cocoa, and cinnamon until blended.

5 ▼ Add the eggs, 1 at a time, beating just enough to blend.

6 Pour into the pie shell and bake on the hot sheet for 25–30 minutes. The filling will sink down as it cools. Decorate with whipped cream and chocolate curls.

Frozen Strawberry Pie

SERVES 8

8 ounces cream cheese

1 cup sour cream

2 10-ounce packages frozen sliced strawberries, thawed

FOR THE CRUST

1¼ cup graham cracker crumbs

1 tablespoon sugar

5 tablespoons butter, melted

1 ▲ For the crust, mix together the crumbs, sugar, and butter.

2 Press the crumbs evenly and firmly over the bottom and sides of a 9-inch pie pan. Freeze until firm.

3 ▼ Blend together the cream cheese and sour cream. Set aside ½ cup of the strawberries and their juice. Add the rest to the cream cheese mixture.

4 Pour the filling into the crust and freeze 6–8 hours until firm. To serve, slice and spoon some of the reserved berries and juice on top.

> **~ VARIATION ~**
>
> For Frozen Raspberry Pie, use raspberries in place of the strawberries and prepare the same way, or try other frozen fruit.

Chocolate Cheesecake Pie (top), Frozen Strawberry Pie

CAKES & TORTES

~

*As tasty as they are beautiful, with homespun charm
or sophisticated style, this selection of classic cheesecakes,
gorgeous coffee cakes, and frosted tortes are simplicity itself
to create and are sure to make any occasion memorable.*

Angel Food Cake

SERVES 12–14

1 cup sifted cake flour
1½ cups superfine sugar
1¼ cups egg whites (about 10–11 eggs)
1¼ teaspoons cream of tartar
¼ teaspoon salt
1 teaspoon vanilla extract
¼ teaspoon almond extract
confectioners' sugar, for dusting

1 Preheat the oven to 325°F.

2 ▼ Sift the flour before measuring, then sift it **4** times with ½ cup of the sugar. Transfer to a bowl.

3 With an electric mixer, beat the egg whites until foamy. Sift over the cream of tartar and salt and continue to beat until they hold soft peaks when the beaters are lifted.

4 ▲ Add the remaining sugar in **3** batches, beating well after each addition. Stir in the vanilla and almond extracts.

5 ▲ Add the flour mixture, ½ cup at a time, and fold in with a large metal spoon after each addition.

6 Transfer to an ungreased 10-inch tube pan and bake until delicately browned on top, about 1 hour.

7 ▲ Turn the pan upside down onto a cake rack and let cool for 1 hour. If the cake does not unmold, run a spatula around the edge to loosen it. Invert on a serving plate.

8 When cool, lay a star-shaped template on top of the cake, sift over confectioners' sugar, and lift off.

Carrot Cake with Maple Butter Frosting

SERVES 12

1 pound carrots, peeled

1½ cups flour

2 teaspoons baking powder

½ teaspoon baking soda

1 teaspoon salt

2 teaspoons ground cinnamon

4 eggs

2 teaspoons vanilla extract

1 cup dark brown sugar, firmly packed

½ cup granulated sugar

1¼ cups sunflower oil

1 cup walnuts, finely chopped

½ cup raisins

walnut halves, for decorating (optional)

FOR THE FROSTING

6 tablespoons unsalted butter, at room
temperature

3 cups confectioners' sugar

¼ cup maple syrup

1 Preheat the oven to 350°F. Line an
11- × 8-inch rectangular baking pan
with wax paper and grease.

2 ▲ Grate the carrots and set aside.

3 Sift the flour, baking powder,
baking soda, salt, and cinnamon into
a bowl. Set aside.

4 With an electric mixer, beat the
eggs until blended. Add the vanilla,
sugars, and oil; beat to incorporate.
Add the dry ingredients, in 3 batches,
folding in well after each addition.

5 ▲ Add the carrots, walnuts, and
raisins and fold in thoroughly.

6 Pour the batter into the prepared
pan and bake until the cake springs
back when touched lightly, 40–45
minutes. Let stand 10 minutes, then
unmold and transfer to a rack.

7 ▼ For the frosting, cream the
butter with half the sugar until soft.
Add the syrup, then beat in the
remaining sugar until blended.

8 Spread the frosting over the top of
the cake. Using a metal spatula, make
decorative ridges across the top. Cut
into squares. Decorate with walnut
halves, if wished.

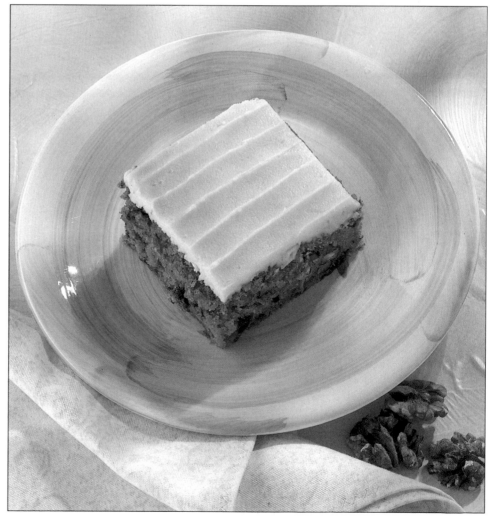

Pecan-Apple Torte

SERVES 8

1 cup pecan halves

½ cup flour

2 teaspoons baking powder

¼ teaspoon salt

2 large cooking apples

3 eggs

1 cup sugar

1 teaspoon vanilla extract

¾ cup whipping cream

1 Preheat the oven to 325°F. Line 2 9-inch cake pans with wax paper and grease. Spread the pecans on a baking sheet and bake for 10 minutes.

2 Finely chop the pecans. Reserve 1½ tablespoons and place the rest in a mixing bowl. Sift over the flour, baking powder, and salt and stir.

3 ▲ Quarter, core, and peel the apples. Cut into ⅛-inch dice, then stir into the pecan-flour mixture.

4 ▲ With an electric mixer, beat the eggs until frothy. Gradually add the sugar and vanilla and beat until a ribbon forms, about 8 minutes. Gently fold in the flour mixture.

5 Pour into the pans and level the tops. Bake until a cake tester inserted in the center comes out clean, about 35 minutes. Let stand 10 minutes.

6 ▲ To loosen, run a knife around the inside edge of each pan. Let cool.

7 ▲ Whip the cream until firm. Spread half over the cake. Top with the second cake. Pipe whipped cream rosettes on top and sprinkle over the reserved pecans before serving.

Spice Cake

SERVES 10–12

1¼ cups milk

2 tablespoons dark corn syrup

2 teaspoons vanilla extract

¾ cup walnuts, chopped

¾ cup (1½ sticks) butter, at room temperature

1½ cups sugar

1 egg, at room temperature

3 egg yolks, at room temperature

2 cups flour

1 tablespoon baking powder

1 teaspoon grated nutmeg

1 teaspoon ground cinnamon

½ teaspoon ground cloves

¼ teaspoon ground ginger

¼ teaspoon ground allspice

FOR THE FROSTING

6 ounces cream cheese

2 tablespoons unsalted butter, at room temperature

1¾ cups confectioners' sugar

2 tablespoons finely chopped stem ginger

2 tablespoons syrup from stem ginger

stem ginger pieces, for decorating

1 Preheat the oven to 350°F. Line 3 8-inch cake pans with wax paper and grease. In a bowl, combine the milk, corn syrup, vanilla, and walnuts.

2 ▼ With an electric mixer, cream the butter and sugar until light and fluffy. Beat in the egg and egg yolks. Add the milk mixture and stir well.

3 Sift together the flour, baking powder and spices 3 times.

4 ▲ Add the flour mixture in 4 batches, and fold in carefully after each addition.

5 Divide the cake mixture between the pans. Bake until the cakes spring back when touched lightly, about 25 minutes. Let stand 5 minutes, then unmold and cool on a rack.

6 ▼ For the frosting, combine all the ingredients and beat with an electric mixer. Spread the frosting between the layers and over the top. Decorate with pieces of stem ginger.

Raspberry-Hazelnut Meringue Cake

SERVES 8

1 cup hazelnuts
4 egg whites
⅛ teaspoon salt
1 cup sugar
½ teaspoon vanilla extract
FOR THE FILLING
1¼ cups whipping cream
1½ pounds raspberries, about 3 pints

1 Preheat the oven to 350°F. Line the bottom of 2 8-inch cake pans with wax paper and grease.

2 Spread the hazelnuts on a baking sheet and bake until lightly toasted, about 8 minutes. Let cool slightly.

3 ▲ Rub the hazelnuts vigorously in a clean dish towel to remove most of the skins.

4 Grind the nuts in a food processor, blender, or nut grinder until they are the consistency of coarse sand.

5 Reduce the oven heat to 300°F.

6 With an electric mixer, beat the egg whites and salt until they hold stiff peaks. Beat in 2 tablespoons of the sugar, then fold in the remaining sugar, a few tablespoons at a time, with a rubber spatula. Fold in the vanilla and the hazelnuts.

7 ▲ Divide the batter between the prepared pans and spread level.

8 Bake for 1¼ hours. If the meringues brown too quickly, protect with a sheet of foil. Let stand 5 minutes, then carefully run a knife around the inside edge of the pans to loosen. Transfer to a rack to cool.

9 For the filling, whip the cream just until firm.

10 ▲ Spread half the cream in an even layer on one meringue round and top with half the raspberries.

11 Top with the other meringue round. Spread the remaining cream on top and arrange the remaining raspberries over the cream. Refrigerate for 1 hour to facilitate cutting.

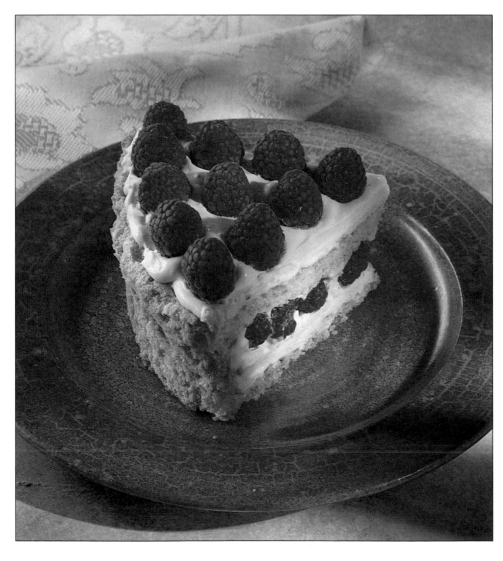

Devil's Food Cake with Orange Frosting

SERVES 8–10

½ cup unsweetened cocoa powder
¾ cup boiling water
¾ cup (1½ sticks) butter, at room temperature
1½ cups dark brown sugar, firmly packed
3 eggs, at room temperature
2 cups flour
1½ teaspoons baking soda
¼ teaspoon baking powder
¾ cup sour cream
orange rind strips, for decoration
FOR THE FROSTING
1½ cups granulated sugar
2 egg whites
4 tablespoons frozen orange juice concentrate
1 tablespoon fresh lemon juice
grated rind of 1 orange

1 Preheat the oven to 350°F. Line 2 9-inch cake pans with wax paper and grease. In a bowl, mix the cocoa and water until smooth. Set aside.

2 With an electric mixer, cream the butter and sugar until light and fluffy. Add the eggs, 1 at a time, beating well after each addition.

3 ▲ When the cocoa mixture is lukewarm, add to the butter mixture.

4 ▼ Sift together the flour, baking soda, and baking powder twice. Fold into the cocoa mixture in 3 batches, alternating with the sour cream.

5 Pour into the pans and bake until the cakes pull away from the sides of the pan, 30–35 minutes. Let stand 15 minutes before unmolding.

6 Thinly slice the orange rind strips. Blanch in boiling water for 1 minute.

7 ▲ For the frosting, place all the ingredients in the top of a double boiler or in a bowl set over hot water. With an electric mixer, beat until the mixture holds soft peaks. Continue beating off the heat until thick enough to spread.

8 Sandwich the cake layers with frosting, then spread over the top and sides. Arrange the blanched orange rind strips on top of the cake.

Sachertorte

SERVES 8–10

2 1-ounce squares semisweet chocolate
2 1-ounce squares unsweetened chocolate
6 tablespoons unsalted butter, at room temperature
½ cup sugar
4 eggs, separated
1 egg white
¼ teaspoon salt
½ cup cake flour, sifted
FOR THE TOPPING
5 tablespoons apricot jam
1 cup plus 1 tablespoon water
1 tablespoon unsalted butter
6 1-ounce squares semisweet chocolate
¾ cup sugar
ready-made chocolate decorating icing (optional)

1 Preheat the oven to 325°F. Line a 9- × 2-inch cake pan with wax paper and grease.

2 ▲ Melt both chocolates in the top of a double boiler, or in a heatproof bowl set over hot water. Set aside.

3 With an electric mixer, cream the butter and sugar until light and fluffy. Stir in the chocolate.

4 ▲ Beat in the yolks, 1 at a time.

5 In another bowl, beat the egg whites with the salt until stiff.

6 ▲ Fold a dollop of whites into the chocolate mixture to lighten it. Fold in the remaining whites in 3 batches, alternating with the sifted flour.

7 ▲ Pour into the pan and bake until a cake tester comes out clean, about 45 minutes. Unmold onto a rack.

8 ▲ Meanwhile, melt the jam with 1 tablespoon of the water over low heat, then strain for a smooth consistency.

9 For the frosting, melt the butter and chocolate in the top of a double boiler or a bowl set over hot water.

10 ▲ In a heavy saucepan, dissolve the sugar in the remaining water over low heat. Raise the heat and boil until the mixture reaches 221°F on a sugar thermometer. Immediately plunge the bottom of the pan into cold water for 1 minute. Pour into the chocolate mixture and stir to blend. Let cool for a few minutes before using.

11 To assemble, brush the warm jam over the cake. Starting in the center, pour over the frosting and work outward in a circular movement. Tilt the rack to spread; only use a spatula for the sides of the cake. Leave to set overnight. If wished, decorate with chocolate icing.

Rich Chocolate Pecan Cake

SERVES 10

1 cup (2 sticks) butter

8 1-ounce squares semisweet chocolate

1 cup unsweetened cocoa powder

1½ cups sugar

6 eggs

⅓ cup brandy or cognac

2 cups pecans, finely chopped

FOR THE GLAZE

4 tablespoons butter

5 1-ounce squares bittersweet chocolate

2 tablespoons milk

1 teaspoon vanilla extract

1 Preheat the oven to 350°F. Line a 9- × 2-inch round cake pan with wax paper and grease.

2 Melt the butter and chocolate together in the top of a double boiler, or in a heatproof bowl set over hot water. Set aside to cool.

3 ▼ Sift the cocoa into a bowl. Add the sugar and eggs and stir until just combined. Pour in the melted chocolate mixture and brandy.

4 Fold in three-quarters of the pecans, then pour the batter into the prepared pan.

5 ▲ Set the pan inside a large pan and pour 1 inch of hot water into the outer pan. Bake until the cake is firm to the touch, about 45 minutes. Let stand 15 minutes, then unmold and transfer to a cooling rack.

6 Wrap the cake in wax paper and refrigerate for at least 6 hours.

7 For the glaze, combine the butter, chocolate, milk, and vanilla in the top of a double boiler or in a heatproof bowl set over hot water, until melted.

8 Place a piece of wax paper under the cake, then drizzle spoonfuls of glaze along the edge; it should drip down and coat the sides. Pour the remaining glaze on top of the cake.

9 ▲ Cover the sides of the cake with the remaining pecans, gently pressing them on with the palm of your hand.

Chocolate Brownie Cake

SERVES 8–10

4 1-ounce squares unsweetened chocolate
¾ cup (1½ sticks) butter
2 cups sugar
3 eggs
1 teaspoon vanilla extract
1½ cups flour
1 teaspoon baking powder
1 cup walnuts, chopped
FOR THE TOPPING
1½ cups whipping cream
8 1-ounce squares semisweet chocolate
1 tablespoon vegetable oil

1 Preheat the oven to 350°F. Line 2 8-inch cake pans with wax paper and grease the paper.

2 Melt the chocolate and butter together in the top of a double boiler, or in a heatproof bowl set over a saucepan of hot water.

3 ▲ Transfer to a mixing bowl and stir in the sugar. Add the eggs and vanilla and mix until well blended.

~ **VARIATION** ~

To make Chocolate Brownie Ice Cream Cake, sandwich the cake layers with softened vanilla ice cream. Freeze until serving.

4 ▲ Sift over the flour and baking powder. Stir in the walnuts.

5 Divide the batter between the prepared pans and spread level.

6 Bake until a cake tester inserted in the center comes out clean, about 30 minutes. Let stand 10 minutes, then unmold and transfer to a rack.

7 When the cakes are cool, whip the cream until firm. With a long serrated knife, carefully slice each cake in half horizontally.

8 Sandwich the layers with some of the whipped cream and spread the remainder over the top of the cake. Refrigerate until needed.

9 ▼ For the chocolate curls, melt the chocolate and oil in the top of a double boiler or a bowl set over hot water. Transfer to a non-porous surface. Spread to a ⅜-inch thick rectangle. Just before the chocolate sets, hold the blade of a straight knife at an angle to the chocolate and scrape across the surface to make curls. Place on top of the cake.

Best-Ever Chocolate Cake

SERVES 12–14

½ cup (1 stick) unsalted butter

1 cup cake flour

½ cup unsweetened cocoa powder

1 teaspoon baking powder

⅛ teaspoon salt

6 eggs

1 cup sugar

2 teaspoons vanilla extract

FOR THE FROSTING

8 1-ounce squares semisweet chocolate, chopped

6 tablespoons unsalted butter

3 eggs, separated

1 cup whipping cream

3 tablespoons sugar

1 Preheat the oven to 350°F. Line 3 8- × 1½-inch round cake pans with wax paper and grease.

2 ▲ Dust evenly with flour and spread with a brush. Set aside.

~ **VARIATION** ~

For a simpler frosting, combine 1 cup whipping cream with 8 ounces finely chopped semisweet chocolate in a saucepan. Stir over low heat until the chocolate has melted. Cool and whisk to spreading consistency.

3 ▲ Melt the butter over low heat. With a spoon, skim off any foam that rises to the surface. Set aside.

4 ▲ Sift the flour, cocoa, baking powder, and salt together 3 times and set aside.

5 Place the eggs and sugar in a large heatproof bowl set over a pan of hot water. With an electric mixer, beat until the mixture doubles in volume and is thick enough to leave a ribbon trail when the beaters are lifted, about 10 minutes. Add the vanilla.

6 ▲ Sift over the dry ingredients in 3 batches, folding in carefully after each addition. Fold in the butter.

7 Divide the batter between the pans and bake until the cakes pull away from the sides of the pan, about 25 minutes. Transfer to a rack.

8 For the frosting, melt the chopped chocolate in the top of a double boiler, or in a heatproof bowl set over hot water.

9 ▲ Off the heat, stir in the butter and egg yolks. Return to low heat and stir until thick. Remove from the heat and set aside.

10 Whip the cream until firm; set aside. In another bowl, beat the egg whites until stiff. Add the sugar and beat until glossy.

11 Fold the cream into the chocolate mixture, then carefully fold in the egg whites. Refrigerate for 20 minutes to thicken the frosting.

12 ▲ Sandwich the cake layers with frosting, stacking them carefully. Spread the remaining frosting evenly over the top and sides of the cake.

Lemon Yogurt Coffee Cake

SERVES 12

1 cup (2 sticks) butter, at room temperature

1½ cups granulated sugar

4 eggs, at room temperature, separated

2 teaspoons grated lemon rind

⅓ cup fresh lemon juice

1 cup plain yogurt

2 cups flour

2 teaspoons baking powder

1 teaspoon baking soda

½ teaspoon salt

FOR THE GLAZE

1 cup confectioners' sugar

2 tablespoons fresh lemon juice

3–4 tablespoons plain yogurt

1 Preheat the oven to 350°F. Grease a 12-cup bundt or tube pan and dust with flour.

2 With an electric mixer, cream the butter and granulated sugar until light and fluffy. Add the egg yolks, 1 at a time, beating well after each addition.

3 ▲ Add the lemon rind, juice, and yogurt and stir to blend.

4 Sift together the flour, baking powder, and baking soda. Set aside. In another bowl, beat the egg whites and salt until they hold stiff peaks.

5 ▲ Fold the dry ingredients into the butter mixture, then fold in a dollop of egg whites. Fold in the remaining whites until blended.

6 Pour into the pan and bake until a cake tester inserted in the center comes out clean, about 50 minutes. Let stand 15 minutes, then unmold and transfer to a cooling rack.

7 For the glaze, sift the confectioners' sugar into a bowl. Stir in the lemon juice and just enough yogurt to make a smooth glaze.

8 ▲ Set the cooled cake on a rack over a sheet of wax paper or a baking sheet. Pour over the glaze and let it drip down the sides. Allow the glaze to set before serving.

Gingerbread

SERVES 8–10

1 tablespoon vinegar
¾ cup milk
1½ cups flour
2 teaspoons baking powder
¼ teaspoon baking soda
½ teaspoon salt
2 teaspoons ground ginger
1 teaspoon ground cinnamon
¼ teaspoon ground cloves
½ cup (1 stick) butter, at room temperature
½ cup sugar
1 egg, at room temperature
¾ cup molasses
whipped cream, for serving
chopped stem ginger, for decorating

1 ▲ Preheat the oven to 350°F. Line the bottom of an 8-inch square cake pan with wax paper and grease the paper and sides of the pan.

2 ▲ Add the vinegar to the milk and set aside. It will curdle.

3 In another mixing bowl, sift all the dry ingredients together 3 times and set aside.

4 With an electric mixer, cream the butter and sugar until light and fluffy. Beat in the egg until well combined.

5 ▼ Stir in the molasses.

6 ▲ Fold in the dry ingredients in 4 batches, alternating with the curdled milk. Mix only enough to blend.

7 Pour into the prepared pan and bake until firm, 45–50 minutes. Cut into squares and serve warm, with whipped cream. Decorate with the stem ginger.

Whiskey Cake

MAKES 1 LOAF

1½ cups walnuts, chopped

½ cup raisins, chopped

½ cup currants

1 cup flour

1 teaspoon baking powder

¼ teaspoon salt

½ cup (1 stick) butter

1 cup sugar

3 eggs, at room temperature, separated

1 teaspoon grated nutmeg

½ teaspoon ground cinnamon

⅓ cup bourbon whiskey

confectioners' sugar, for dusting

1 ▼ Preheat the oven to 325°F. Line the bottom of a 9- × 5- × 3-inch loaf pan with wax paper and grease the paper and sides of the pan.

2 ▲ Place the walnuts, raisins, and currants in a bowl. Sprinkle over 2 tablespoons of the flour, mix and set aside. Sift together the remaining flour, baking powder, and salt.

3 ▲ Cream the butter and sugar until light and fluffy. Beat in the egg yolks.

4 Mix the nutmeg, cinnamon, and whiskey. Fold into the butter mixture, alternating with the flour mixture.

5 ▲ In another bowl, beat the egg whites until stiff. Fold into the whiskey mixture until just blended. Fold in the walnut mixture.

6 Bake until a cake tester inserted in the center comes out clean, about 1 hour. Let cool in the pan. Dust with confectioners' sugar over a template.

Dark Fruit Cake

SERVES 12

1 cup currants

1 cup raisins

⅔ cup golden raisins

¼ cup candied cherries, halved

3 tablespoons Madeira or sherry wine

¾ cup (1½ sticks) butter

1 cup dark brown sugar, firmly packed

2 extra-large eggs, at room temperature

1⅔ cups flour

2 teaspoons baking powder

2 teaspoons each ground ginger, allspice, and cinnamon

1 tablespoon dark corn syrup

1 tablespoon milk

¼ cup mixed candied fruit, chopped

1 cup walnuts or pecans, chopped

FOR THE DECORATION

1 cup sugar

½ cup water

1 lemon, thinly sliced

½ orange, thinly sliced

½ cup orange marmalade

candied cherries

1 One day before preparing, combine the currants, both raisins, and the cherries in a bowl. Stir in the Madeira or sherry. Cover and let stand overnight to macerate.

2 Preheat the oven to 300°F. Line a 9- × 3-inch springform pan with wax paper and grease. Place a tray of hot water on the bottom of the oven.

3 With an electric mixer, cream the butter and sugar until light and fluffy. Beat in the eggs, 1 at a time.

4 ▲ Sift the flour, baking powder, and spices together 3 times. Fold into the butter mixture in 3 batches. Fold in the corn syrup, milk, dried fruit and liquid, candied fruit, and nuts.

5 ▲ Spoon into the pan, spreading out so there is a slight depression in the center of the batter.

6 Bake until a cake tester inserted in the center comes out clean, 2½–3 hours. Cover with foil when the top is golden to prevent overbrowning. Cool in the pan on a rack.

7 ▲ For the decoration, combine the sugar and water in a saucepan and bring to a boil. Add the lemon and orange slices and cook until candied, about 20 minutes. Work in batches, if necessary. Remove the fruit with a slotted spoon. Pour the remaining syrup over the cake and let cool. Melt the marmalade over low heat, then brush over the top of the cake. Decorate with the candied citrus slices and cherries.

Heart Cake

MAKES 1 CAKE

1 cup (2 sticks) butter or margarine, at room temperature
1 cup sugar
4 eggs, at room temperature
1½ cups flour
1 teaspoon baking powder
½ teaspoon baking soda
2 tablespoons milk
1 teaspoon vanilla extract

FOR FROSTING AND DECORATING

3 egg whites
1½ cups granulated sugar
2 tablespoons cold water
2 tablespoons fresh lemon juice
¼ teaspoon cream of tartar
pink food coloring
¾–1 cup confectioners' sugar

1 Preheat the oven to 350°F. Line an 8-inch heart-shaped cake pan with wax paper and grease.

2 ▲ With an electric mixer, cream the butter or margarine and sugar until light and fluffy. Add the eggs, 1 at a time, beating thoroughly after each addition.

3 Sift the flour, baking powder, and baking soda together. Fold the dry ingredients into the butter mixture in 3 batches, alternating with the milk. Stir in the vanilla.

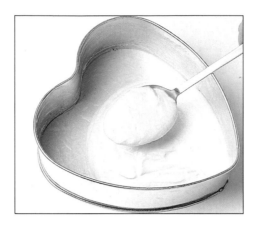

4 ▲ Spoon the batter into the prepared pan and bake until a cake tester inserted in the center comes out clean, 35–40 minutes. Let the cake stand in the pan for 5 minutes, then unmold and transfer to a rack to cool completely.

5 For the frosting, combine 2 of the egg whites, the granulated sugar, water, lemon juice, and cream of tartar in the top of a double boiler or in a bowl set over simmering water. With an electric mixer, beat until thick and holds soft peaks, about 7 minutes. Remove from the heat and continue beating until the mixture is thick enough to spread. Tint the frosting with the pink food coloring.

6 ▲ Put the cake on a board, about 12 inches square, covered in foil or in paper suitable for contact with food. Spread the frosting evenly on the cake. Smooth the top and sides. Leave to set 3–4 hours, or overnight.

7 ▲ For the paper piping bags, fold an 11- × 8-inch sheet of parchment or wax paper in half diagonally, then cut into 2 pieces along the fold mark. Roll over the short side, so that it meets the right-angled corner and forms a cone. To form the piping bag, hold the cone in place with one hand, wrap the point of the long side of the triangle around the cone, and tuck inside, folding over twice to secure. Snip a hole in the pointed end and slip in a small metal piping tip to extend about ¼ inch.

8 For the piped decorations, place 1 tablespoon of the remaining egg white in a bowl and whisk until frothy. Gradually beat in enough confectioners' sugar to make a stiff mixture suitable for piping.

9 ▲ Spoon into a paper piping bag to half-fill. Fold over the top and squeeze to pipe decorations on the top and sides of the cake.

Cup Cakes

MAKES 16

½ cup (1 stick) butter, at room temperature

1 cup granulated sugar

2 eggs, at room temperature

1½ cups cake flour

¼ teaspoon salt

1½ teaspoons baking powder

½ cup plus 1 tablespoon milk

1 teaspoon vanilla extract

FOR FROSTING AND DECORATING

2 large egg whites

3½ cups sifted confectioners' sugar

1–2 drops glycerin

juice of 1 lemon

food colorings

colored sprinkles, for decorating

candied lemon and orange slices, for decorating

1 Preheat the oven to 375°F.

2 ▲ Fill 16 muffin cups with fluted paper baking liners, or grease.

~ **COOK'S TIP** ~

Ready-made cake decorating products are widely available, and may be used, if preferred, instead of the recipes given for frosting and decorating. Colored gel in tubes with piping tips is useful.

3 With an electric mixer, cream the butter and sugar until light and fluffy. Add the eggs, 1 at a time, beating well after each addition.

4 Sift together the flour, salt, and baking powder. Stir into the butter mixture, alternating with the milk. Stir in the vanilla.

5 ▲ Fill the cups half-full and bake until the tops spring back when touched lightly, about 20 minutes. Let the cup cakes stand in the pan for 5 minutes, then unmold and transfer to a rack to cool completely.

6 For the meringue frosting, beat the egg whites until stiff but not dry. Gradually add the sugar, glycerin, and lemon juice, and continue beating for 1 minute. The consistency should be spreadable. If necessary, thin with a little water or add more sifted confectioners' sugar.

7 ▲ Divide the frosting between several bowls and tint with food colorings. Spread different colored frostings over the cooled cup cakes.

8 ▲ Decorate the cup cakes as wished, such as with different colored sprinkles.

9 ▲ Other decorations include candied orange and lemon slices. Cut into small pieces and arrange on top of the cup cakes. Alternatively, use other suitable candies.

10 ▲ To decorate with colored frostings, fill paper piping bags with different colored frostings. Pipe on faces, or make other designs.

Walnut Coffee Torte

SERVES 8–10

1¼ cups walnuts
¾ cup sugar
5 eggs, separated
⅓ cup dry bread crumbs
1 tablespoon unsweetened cocoa powder
1 tablespoon instant coffee
2 tablespoons rum or lemon juice
⅛ teaspoon salt
6 tablespoons concord grape or red currant jelly
chopped walnuts, for decorating
FOR THE FROSTING
8 1-ounce squares bittersweet chocolate
3 cups whipping cream

3 ▲ Grind the nuts with 3 tablespoons of the sugar in a food processor, blender, or nut grinder.

4 With an electric mixer, beat the egg yolks and remaining sugar until thick and lemon-colored.

5 ▲ Fold in the walnuts. Stir in the bread crumbs, cocoa, coffee, and rum or lemon juice.

6 ▲ In another bowl, beat the egg whites with the salt until they hold stiff peaks. Fold carefully into the walnut mixture with a rubber spatula.

7 Pour the meringue batter into the prepared pan and bake until the top of the cake springs back when touched lightly, about 45 minutes. Let the cake stand for 5 minutes, then unmold and transfer to a rack.

8 ▲ When cool, slice the cake in half horizontally.

9 With an electric mixer, beat the chocolate frosting mixture on low speed until it becomes lighter, about 30 seconds. Do not overbeat or it may become grainy.

10 ▲ Warm the jelly in a saucepan until melted, then brush over the cut cake layer. Spread with some of the chocolate frosting, then sandwich with the remaining cake layer. Brush the top of the cake with jelly, then cover the sides and top with the remaining chocolate frosting. Make a starburst pattern by pressing gently with a table knife in lines radiating from the center. Sprinkle the chopped walnuts around the edge.

1 ▲ For the frosting, combine the chocolate and cream in the top of a double boiler, or in a heatproof bowl set over simmering water. Stir until the chocolate dissolves. Let cool, then cover and refrigerate until the mixture is firm, or overnight.

2 Preheat the oven to 350°F. Line a 9- × 2-inch cake pan with wax paper and grease.

Chiffon Cake

SERVES 16

2 cups flour

1 tablespoon baking powder

1 teaspoon salt

1½ cups sugar

½ cup vegetable oil

7 eggs, at room temperature, separated

¾ cup cold water

2 teaspoons vanilla extract

2 teaspoons grated lemon rind

½ teaspoon cream of tartar

FOR THE FROSTING

⅔ cup (10⅔ tablespoons) unsalted butter, at room temperature

5 cups confectioners' sugar

4 teaspoons instant coffee dissolved in 4 tablespoons hot water

1 Preheat the oven to 325°F.

2 ▼ Sift the flour, baking powder, and salt into a bowl. Stir in 1 cup of the sugar. Make a well in the center and add in the following order: oil, egg yolks, water, vanilla, and lemon rind. Beat with a whisk or metal spoon until the mixture is smooth.

3 With an electric mixer, beat the egg whites with the cream of tartar until they hold soft peaks. Add the remaining ½ cup of sugar and beat until they hold stiff peaks.

4 ▲ Pour the flour mixture over the whites in 3 batches, folding well after each addition.

5 Transfer the batter to an ungreased 10- × 4-inch tube pan and bake until the top springs back when touched lightly, about 1 hour and 10 minutes.

6 ▲ When baked, remove from the oven and immediately hang the cake upside-down over the neck of a funnel or a narrow bottle. Let cool. To remove the cake, run a knife around the inside to loosen, then turn the pan over and tap the sides sharply. Invert the cake onto a serving plate.

7 For the frosting, beat together the butter and confectioners' sugar with an electric mixer until smooth. Add the coffee and beat until fluffy. With a metal spatula, spread over the sides and top of the cake.

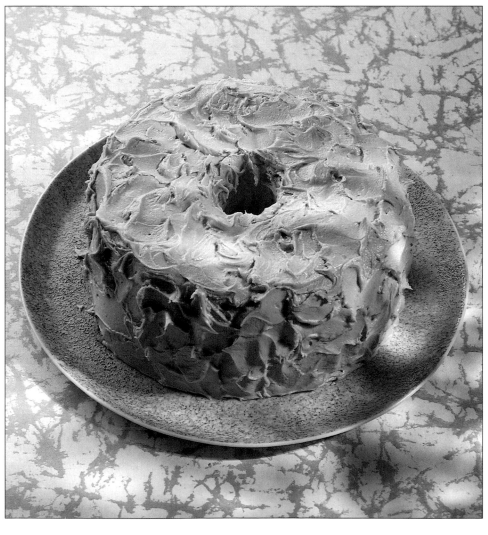

Black and White Pound Cake

SERVES 16

4 1-ounce squares semisweet chocolate

3 cups flour

1 teaspoon baking powder

2 cups (4 sticks) butter, at room temperature

3⅓ cups sugar

1 tablespoon vanilla extract

10 eggs, at room temperature

confectioners' sugar, for dusting

1 ▲ Preheat the oven to 350°F. Line the bottom of a 10-inch tube pan with wax paper and grease. Dust with flour and spread evenly with a brush.

2 ▲ Melt the chocolate in the top of a double boiler, or in a heatproof bowl set over a pan of hot water. Stir occasionally. Set aside.

3 In a bowl, sift together the flour and baking powder. In another bowl, cream the butter, sugar, and vanilla with an electric mixer until light and fluffy. Add the eggs, 2 at a time, then gradually incorporate the flour mixture on low speed.

4 ▲ Spoon half of the batter into the prepared pan.

5 ▲ Stir the chocolate into the remaining batter, then spoon into the pan. With a metal spatula, swirl the two batters to create a marbled effect.

6 Bake until a cake tester inserted in the center comes out clean, about 1 hour 45 minutes. Cover with foil halfway through baking. Let stand 15 minutes, then unmold and transfer to a cooling rack. To serve, dust with confectioners' sugar.

Lady Baltimore Cake

SERVES 8–10

2½ cups flour

2½ teaspoons baking powder

½ teaspoon salt

4 eggs

1½ cups sugar

grated rind of 1 large orange

1 cup freshly squeezed orange juice

1 cup vegetable oil

FOR THE FROSTING

2 egg whites

1½ cup sugar

5 tablespoons cold water

¼ teaspoon cream of tartar

1 teaspoon vanilla extract

½ cup pecans, finely chopped

½ cup raisins, chopped

3 dried figs, finely chopped

18 pecan halves, for decorating

1 Preheat the oven to 350°F. Line 2 9-inch round cake pans with wax paper and grease.

2 In a bowl, sift together the flour, baking powder, and salt. Set aside.

3 ▲ With an electric mixer, beat the eggs and sugar until thick and lemon-colored. Beat in the orange rind and juice, then the oil.

4 On low speed beat in the flour mixture in 3 batches. Divide the batter between the prepared pans.

5 ▲ Bake until a cake tester inserted in the center comes out clean, about 30 minutes. Let stand 15 minutes. To unmold, run a knife around the inside edge, then transfer the cakes to racks to cool completely.

6 ▲ For the frosting, combine the egg whites, sugar, water, and cream of tartar in the top of a double boiler, or in a heatproof bowl set over boiling water. With an electric mixer, beat until glossy and thick. Off the heat, add the vanilla, and continue beating until thick. Fold in the pecans, raisins, and figs.

7 Spread a layer of frosting on top of one cake. Sandwich with the second cake, then spread the top and sides with the rest of the frosting. Arrange the pecan halves on top.

Sour Cream Streusel Coffee Cake

SERVES 12–14

½ cup (1 stick) butter, at room temperature

⅔ cup granulated sugar

3 eggs, at room temperature

1½ cups flour

1 teaspoon baking soda

1 teaspoon baking powder

1 cup sour cream

FOR THE TOPPING

1 cup dark brown sugar, firmly packed

2 teaspoons ground cinnamon

1 cup walnuts, finely chopped

4 tablespoons cold butter, cut in pieces

1 Preheat the oven to 350°F. Line the bottom of a 9-inch square cake pan with wax paper and grease.

2 ▲ For the topping, place the brown sugar, cinnamon, and walnuts in a bowl. Mix with your fingertips, then add the butter and continue working with your fingertips until the mixture resembles coarse crumbs.

3 To make the cake, cream the butter with an electric mixer until soft. Add the sugar and continue beating until the mixture is light and fluffy.

4 Add the eggs, 1 at a time, beating well after each addition.

5 In another bowl, sift the flour, baking soda, and baking powder together 3 times.

6 ▲ Fold the dry ingredients into the butter mixture in 3 batches, alternating with the sour cream. Fold until blended after each addition.

7 ▲ Pour half of the batter into the prepared pan and sprinkle over half of the walnut topping mixture.

8 Pour the remaining batter on top and sprinkle over the remaining walnut mixture.

9 Bake until browned, 60–70 minutes. Let stand 5 minutes, then unmold and transfer to a cooling rack.

Classic Cheesecake

SERVES 8

½ cup graham cracker crumbs

2 pounds cream cheese, at room temperature

1¼ cups sugar

grated rind of 1 lemon

3 tablespoons fresh lemon juice

1 teapoon vanilla extract

4 eggs, at room temperature

1 Preheat the oven to 325°F. Grease an 8-inch springform pan. Place on a round of foil 4–5 inches larger than the diameter of the pan. Press it up the sides to seal tightly.

2 Sprinkle the crumbs in the base of the pan. Press to form an even layer.

3 With an electric mixer, beat the cream cheese until smooth. Add the sugar, lemon rind and juice, and vanilla, and beat until blended. Beat in the eggs, 1 at a time. Beat just enough to blend thoroughly.

4 ▲ Pour into the prepared pan. Set the pan in a larger baking pan and place in the oven. Pour enough hot water in the outer pan to come 1 inch up the side of the pan.

5 Bake until the top of the cake is golden brown, about 1½ hours. Let cool in the pan.

6 ▼ Run a knife around the edge to loosen, then remove the rim of the pan. Refrigerate for at least 4 hours before serving.

Chocolate Cheesecake

SERVES 10–12

6 1-ounce squares semisweet chocolate

4 1-ounce squares unsweetened chocolate

2½ pounds cream cheese, at room temperature

1 cup sugar

2 teaspoons vanilla extract

4 eggs, at room temperature

¾ cup sour cream

FOR THE CRUST

1½ cups chocolate wafer crumbs

6 tablespoons butter, melted

½ teaspoon ground cinnamon

1 Preheat the oven to 350°F. Grease the bottom and sides of a 9- × 3-inch springform pan.

2 ▲ For the crust, mix the chocolate crumbs with the butter and cinnamon. Press evenly in the bottom of the pan.

3 Melt both chocolates in the top of a double boiler, or in a heatproof bowl set over hot water. Set aside.

4 With an electric mixer, beat the cream cheese until smooth, then beat in the sugar and vanilla. Add the eggs, 1 at a time, scraping the bowl with a spatula when necessary.

5 Add the sour cream. Stir in the melted chocolate.

6 ▼ Pour into the crust. Bake for 1 hour. Let cool in the pan; remove rim. Refrigerate before serving.

Classic Cheesecake (top), Chocolate Cheesecake

Lemon Mousse Cheesecake

SERVES 10–12

2½ pounds cream cheese, at room
    temperature

1½ cups sugar

⅓ cup flour

4 eggs, at room temperature, separated

½ cup fresh lemon juice

grated rind of 2 lemons

1 cup graham cracker crumbs

1 Preheat the oven to 325°F. Line a
10- × 2-inch round cake pan with
wax paper and grease.

2 With an electric mixer, beat the
cream cheese until smooth. Gradually
add 1¼ cups of the sugar, and beat
until light. Beat in the flour.

3 ▲ Add the egg yolks, and lemon
juice and rind, and beat until smooth
and well blended.

4 In another bowl, beat the egg
whites until they hold soft peaks. Add
the remaining sugar and beat until stiff
and glossy.

5 ▲ Add the egg whites to the
cheese mixture and gently fold in.

6 Pour the batter into the prepared
pan, then place the pan in a larger
baking pan. Place in the oven and
pour hot water in the outer pan to
come 1 inch up the side.

7 Bake until golden, 60–65 minutes.
Let cool in the pan on a rack. Cover
and refrigerate for at least 4 hours.

8 To unmold, run a knife around the
inside edge. Place a flat plate, bottom-
side up, over the pan and invert onto
the plate. Smooth the top with a
metal spatula.

9 ▲ Sprinkle the crumbs over the
top in an even layer, pressing down
slightly to make a top crust.

10 To serve, cut slices with a sharp
knife dipped in hot water.

INDEX

~